OM

śrī Gaṇeśāya namaḥ

The Indus Aryans and Vedic Culture

Madhusudan Mishra
M.A., Ph.D., Diploma in Applied Linguistics

SHIPRA

ISBN: 81-7541-157-0

First Published in India in 2004

The Indus Aryans and Vedic Culture

Published by :
SHIPRA PUBLICATIONS
115-A, Vikas Marg, Shakarpur,
Delhi-110092 (India)
Ph: 22458662, 22500954 Fax : 91-11-22458662
Email : info@shiprapublications.com
www.shiprapublications.com

Laser Typeset by:
Manas Enterprises
Delhi-110032

Printed at:
Chaudhary Offset Process,
Delhi-110051

एतद्देशप्रसूतस्य सकाशादग्रजन्मनः।
स्वं स्वं चरित्रं शिक्षेरन् पृथिव्यां सर्वमानवाः।।

(मनुस्मृति)

From the elders born in this country, let all human beings on the earth learn their character.

Preface

This book was ready for the press many days before its predecessor, '*The Ṛgveda in the Indus Inscriptions*' had appeared. But it had to wait for its publication, thanks to our various limitations.

Because its predecessor could not be the last work of the author, this too may be followed by some work on the subject. And it may go on.

The readers of this book are requested to read every essay in isolation. As the customary ritual, I thank Sri Nalin Sharma for his bringing it out in immediate succession.

Rāma Navamī **Madhusudan Mishra**
11-4-2003

Contents

Introduction

This book requires no introduction, because its chapters were written independently at unequal intervals without any intention of joining them together later on. That is why, the introduction itself is likely to become an independent chapter, saying something more and something other than what runs between the lines of the different chapters.

Now I am bold enough to assert that I have seen a human speech evolving before my own eyes. As I peep into the dim light of the remote antiquity, I see through my mind's eye the cavemen coming out in the open countryside and facing the catastrophes of the nature. I also hear their babbling turning into articulate human sounds. Now, when they heard a peacock clucking at the top of a tree, they found that it uttered their own ka-sound. They said: ka, meaning 'it clucks'. Later this clucking bird itself was named ka. The same ka of their speech echoed in some animal, reptile, physical object, etc., and their 'state' or 'activity' was referred to as ka. There were as many 'states' or 'activities' as the 'beings' and 'objects' with reference to this single ka. For example:

turtle	:	moves slowly
fire	:	burns
sun	:	shines
air	:	blows
time	:	goes, etc.

This was the case with all the phonemes they had in their

speech. It is possible to pinpoint the state or activity of the object or being with reference to every sound, but it requires a great amount of diligence to verify them.

Some phonemes of their speech were just 'noise' or vague sounds, which were later designated 'svara' (vowel), but many others were clearly articulated (vyakta) sounds, later designated 'vyañjana' (consonant). The consonants could not be pronounced without the help of the vowels. That is why, the exact meaning of vowel (svara) has not been properly understood by many till today. The one is blind and the other is lame, but they walk unfaulteringly together.

As far as imaginable from the oldest list of phonemes under the name of the Māheśvarasūtras, they had 34 consonants and 14 vowels in their speech. At least the vowels a ā i ī u ū e ē o ō were certainly there in the beginning, the diphthongs ai āi au āu developing later. These gave birth to 476 syllables. With this limited wealth of syllables, which were the words of their language, they started communicating with one another. These monosyllabic words stood for all the possible objects and beings in their surroundings.

To be specific about the community speaking this language, it may be said that they were the socalled Indus Aryan people. Initially they had settled on the banks of the river which was later called Sarasvatī. Their descendants conceived that their speech had flowed along the course of that river, which was later deified as 'the goddess of speech.'

They spread far and wide from there. They saw the fire caused by the rubbing of the branches of the sarala-trees in the windy hot summer and said; ra (it burns). The trill of r matched very well with the rattling of the fire, which was named ra. They saw it spreading rapidly in the forest and again said: ra (it runs). They saw a river and said : na (it flows). They saw another river flowing with indistinct noise, and they added one more idea; na da (it flows and makes indistinct noise). They saw a fish and said : ma (it swims). All the verbs later began to refer to the objects. There were as many verbs as objects and beings. The syllables were the same, but their referends were many without any chance of clash, because the referends were only one from the birds one from the animals, one from the reptiles, and so on.

They experienced a long chilly winter, followed by the pleasant spring, the hot summer, the wet rains, the humid autumn and, again, the same chilly winter. The length of their utterance increased. It was now the being and the activity, the object and the state, the subject and the verb. They said: la ṭha (the time turns round). Their speech had no grammar. The specific position of the monosyllabic words showed which was the subject and which was the verb, though this order was itself broken to convey specific idea: gā va (goes into-the-pen). Like the same man doing all functions in the society, the same word served as all parts of speech. It was the stage of the language now called 'isolating'.

At this stage of the language, even if they peeped back into the past and saw the future ahead, they were content with their present, which was their only means of expression. They knew something about the origin of the universe, and said: ṣa ṭha (an egg rolled forth). However, the requirements of the social life were putting pressure on them to invent new ways of expression for the past and future, specially because the life was urbanised. Also important for them was the preservation of the knowledge handed down by their forefathers. Because every syllable of their speech was the name of some animal, bird, reptile, physical object, etc., they just portrayed them for the syllables: la ṭha. This became the textbook of every house in the society. It went on for a long time. In the meanwhile, the animal figures gradually passed into geometrical figures, and then into numerals. It was probably an exercise of several centuries. They began to mix the three writing systems as convenient for them:

ṇa ga
ṣa ṭha

These texts have been handed down to us as found in the ruins of that ancient culture. It is supposed that the urban culture ultimately collapsed. We do not have any idea of what happened after this tragedy. But, fortunately, these texts are traceable in the inflexional language of the RV in their reduced and mutilated forms.

la ṭha : ṛtá (the regular order of the universe)
ṇa ga : nág (night)
ṣa ṭha : sát (the rolling egg)

If we can gauge the length of time between the clause of the isolating stage and the reduced vocable of the inflexional stage, we can point to the time of the writing of the inscriptions, even when the RV is ludicrously put at 1200 BC. At least a stanza of the RV (7,103,9) takes us back to 7000 BC on astronomical grounds, but it is difficult to convince a historian or archaeologist who may go into coma after hearing this ancient date. For an Indian, however, even a stupendously ancient period is just 'yesterday'.

It is remarkable that the agglutinative stage, which is supposed to precede the inflexional Vedic, has completely gone unrecorded. But we can have some idea of that stage by comparing the isolating Indus and the inflexional Vedic.

Though the Indus society faced the tragedy just at the fag end of the isolating stage of the language, there are traces of the agglutinative stage coming into being. But because it was the very early phase of the agglutinative stage, there could not be any uniformity in the languages of the dispersing communities. That is why, the socalled Aryan, (northern), Dravidian (southern) and Munda (central) groups of languages differ widely. While the Dravidian and Munda languages have been marking time at the agglutinative stage, the Aryan languages show their climb down from the inflexional stage. In the unfavourable conditions of the nature, the Dravidian and Munda languages have been limping at the agglutinative stage, while the ancestor of the Aryan languages had reached the inflexional stage. That is why, if these three languages agree at all, it is only on the first syllable of the form. On the whole, they are exotic to one another.

The agglutinative form of Indus, which proceeded towards the inflexional stage, can be imagined through the Vedic. At this stage the father, pointing to his own old father, said to his son : tata ma-ha = father time-perfect (my father has grown old). He was tatā-maha to his grandson. This grandson would then request his grandfather to tell some story, who used to narrate some old events. At the end, the grandfather used to say; iti ha ā-ṣa = thus, say, past-be (thus, they say, it was). We know, how the word itihāsa has come into being.

The river Sarasvatī, which is extolled so eloquently in the RV, flowing mightily at the time of its composition, was not known to the writers of the Indus inscriptions by a name. They saw it and said : ṣa ra ṣa 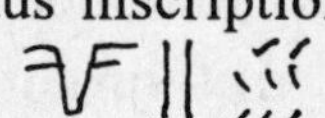 (from the mountain flows and stops at the sea). It was a very long river. When this clause contracted as the phrase sarasa (flowing from the mountain and stopping at the sea) and was reduced to a lexeme sáras (a pond), which characterised the bed of the river from the point of its origin to the place of its rest and was responsible for the name Saras-vat-ī (abounding in ponds), thousands of years had gone by. When the hymns of the RV were being composed, it was the third, the inflexional stage of the language. Our historians and archaeologists compress all these events within a few hundred years.

When the Sanskrit grammarians define a sentence as "eka-tiṅ vākyam" (the sentence has a verb) or when when they etymologise go (cow) as "gacchati iti gauḥ" (a cow is so called because she goes), they do not have only the Sanskrit language in their mind. As a matter of fact, they go to the very origin of the pastoral culture, when a cow was seen entering the pen everyday towards the evening. They define these terms from the cultural point of view, because in the language is their culture.

Though the Sanskrit grammarians are seen explaining 'go' (cow) as 'gacchati' (goes), they certainly knew the initial gā (goes) and the following va (into the pen) from the tradition, which had contracted as g-o, now explained as g(am) + (ḍ) o. That is to say, the Sanskrit grammarians knew the isolating clause gā va (goes into the pen) through the unbroken tradition which, through the agglutinative pl. form gāva-ṣa had turned up as gāvas at the inflexional stage, from which the strong base gāu- was deduced. The weak base gau- (in gav-ā,etc.) and the middle base go- (in go-bhis, etc.) were conceived later. They were careful not to create a hoax like the IE form for 'cow'. This IE has really killed the 'Historical Linguistics'.

A brief outline of the isolating language of the extent

Indus inscriptions having already been given, it is desirable to give a reconstructed picture of the missing agglutinative stage and its transition into the inflexional Vedic.

By the time the writing of the inscriptions had started, the isolating Indus had already transited into the agglutinative stage with the emergence of the future affix gha and the injunctive affix ga. Later on, ha also emerged to show duality and ṣa to show plurality :

ṇara	ṇara-ha	ṇara-ṣa
gāva	gāva-ha	gāva-ṣa

Then -ma came to show the object and -ti to express the oblique cases. The oblique cases too were further distinguished: there was -na for instrumental, -ya for dative, -sa (also extended to s-ya) for possessive, and -si for locative. Then -ti was restricted for ablative. Probably -su was conceived for the locative plural. Various syllables assumed the offices of pronouns in various cases.

mā = me, me = to me, my, mine

tvā = you, te = to you, thy, thine

The verbs show the greater flowering of forms :

(1) the past prefix ā- : ā-ha (past-say)= said, ā-ṣa (past-be) = was

(2) The perfect suffix -ha: ma-ha (time-perfect) has grown old.

(3) the pluperfect affix -ra; ca-ra (be-pluperfect) = had been. The comparative suffix- tara in Vedic is some original pluperfect form, meaning 'had surpassed'

(4) the past suffix -ṭha: ṣa-ṭha (be-past), also contracted as ṣ-ṭha (RV 7,103,9).

-ma: sa-ma, later contracted as s-ma, turning present into past in Sanskrit. Even the superlative suffix -tama is a past form.

In the next phase of the agglutinative stage, the persons were distinguished in the past tense. Keeping the prefix ā intact, -ta was added for the 3rd person. -sa for the 2nd person, and -ma for the 1st person :

3. ā-gā-ta   2. ā-gā-sa   1. ā-gā-ma

When the past was distinguished person-wise, the present tense too distinguished persons by slightly bending a towards i:

3. gā-ti   2.gā-si   1.gā-mi

For the imperative mood, 3. gā-tu was conceived by a slight bending towards u.

Later, even the numbers began to be distinguished. The suffix was the same -ṣa, but the verbal base a- was bent towards u:

ā-ha : ā-hu-ṣa   ā-ṣa : ā-ṣu-ṣa

Otherwise, the plurality was also shown in verbs by inserting -n-: yā-ti sg. ya-n-ti pl.

Generally, the past prefix ā began to be shortened to a. The monosyllabic verbs began to be extended by various syllables: ga became gā,ga-ma, ga-cha, ga-da, ga-ra, etc.

A paragraph in the various phases of the agglutinative Indus may be presented :

ṇara ā-ha : dra-gha ra-ga = A man said: there will be conflagration: do run away!

iha gāva-ṣa ā-ṣu-ṣa = There were cattle here.

ṇara-ṣa ā-hu-ṣa = People said

tata ma-ha = The father has grown old.

mraga ku ca-ra = There had been beast on the earth.

pari ṣa-ṭha = Around be-past

sa pra-cha-ti = He comes forward (to ask).

ajha a-gā-ma = I went.

gāva-ṣa a-gu-ṣa = The cows went.

When the agglutinative Indus came to maturity, it was the spring time of its morphology. The monotony of the language went away and it became accented. Gradually, the flowers dropped down and sweet fruits emerged out. Then

ṇaraṣa	became	náras
ṇamaṣa		námas
tanaṣa		tánas
gāvaṣa		gāvas
ṇaraha		narā from naraH
gāvaha		gāvā from gāvaH
āṣa		ās (RV 10,129,3)
ṣaṭha contracted as		ṣ-ṭha (RV 7,103,9)

maha became the secondary suffix-maha (P. 4,2,36)

cara	-cara (P. 5,3,53)

From gāvas etc. the bases gāu,gau-,go-were deduced. Sometimes the whole phrase contracted as an adjective of obscure meaning : kucara. From tánas, the verb tan and later even tarṣ were deduced. The infixed nasal classes of verbs are the children of this little vocable, which was almost on the death-bed in the language of the RV (5,70,4)

1

The Linguistic Darwinism and the Indus Inscriptions

The discovery of the Indus inscriptions, nineteen-twenties onwards, gave rise to great speculations about the language and script of the texts. Though, by the end of the last decade of the last century, I had been able to identify the language and to partly decode the script, that has not gained favourable comments. There is a tendency not engage in discussion but to dismiss a solution.

It was really certain doubts and querries in my mind which brought me near the success which I claim. I had certain querries on certain expressions of the language of the village dialects which did not belong to any language known to me. Even some Sanskrit particles like kila (it is said), ced (if you say), etc., compressing some whole clauses, seemed to come from some ancient language. Some statements of Pāṇini seemed to suggest that he was aware of some prehistoric primitive language.

The discovery of the Indus inscriptions at least assured me about the existence of such prehistoric language. Though this fact was known to any body, my insight led me to connect the earliest form of Sanskrit with this prehistoric language. That is to say, I had moved one step forward towards its identity. If these particles of Sanskrit or the expression of the village dialects were a part of some borrowing, the creditor was nowhere to be seen. If it was a part of some heritage, the ancestor appeared to lie in the ruins of the excavation. It just required the true identification of the ancestor.

The immediate source of that identification could be the script itself. When analysed, it ran into less than a thousand, which is a characteristics of the logographic script, each symbol standing for some word. But some symbols of the script clearly portray some animals, birds, insects or some physical object; e.g.  mountain,  bee, 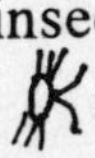 spider, etc., to quote a few definite ones. Referring to the monosyllabic words of the traditional Sanskrit lexicons, compiled in the modern Sanskrit dictionaries, we find that da means 'mountain', bha means 'bee', ba means 'spider' and so on. As a first step towards decipherment, the mountain-sign was read da, the bee-sign was read bha, and the spider-sign was read ba. A rimmed vessel or jar-sign 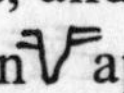 appeared like a nipple of the animal's udder, which was identified as ṣa. Thus, after some exercise, a dozen of signs were provisionally identified as representing some syllables with the vowel a. But it was of no help in saying anything about the language of the inscriptions.

Once, while going through the concordance of the Indus texts, the same text appeared to be in the numeral and geometrical shape of the script in the middle.

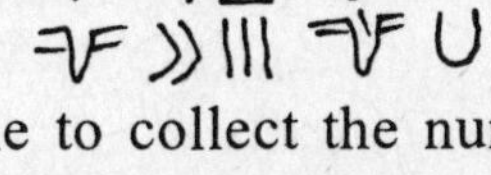

It inspired me to collect the numeral signs of different shapes and lengths at one place:

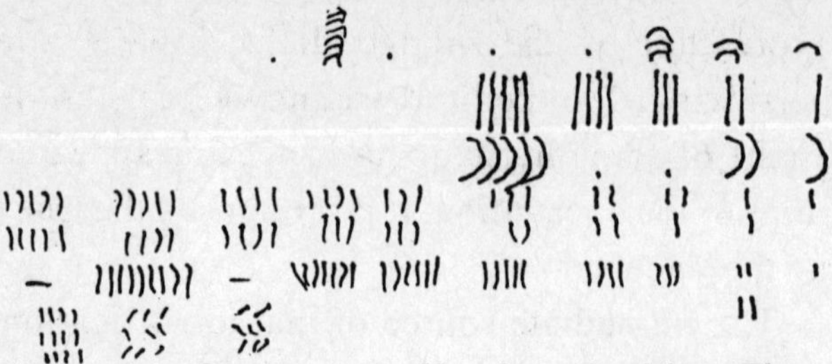

The missing numerals are easily imaginable. They appeared to represent certain order of sounds in numerical way and, guided by some inner voice, I covered them with the syllabic order of the Māheśvarasūtras at the beginning of the Pāṇini's grammar. The covering was so exact that the numerals could be read through that syllabic order. It appeared to say that the syllabary used by Sanskrit really belongs to the language of the Indus inscriptions. It also suggested that the language of the Indus inscriptions and Sanskrit are probably genetically related.

With the help of the numerals, in duplicate and triplicate texts, the other varieties of the script were gradually recognised. It was seen that the texts represent three scripts; a. the animal figures, with which the writing would have started; b. the geometrical figures, which were the natural development from the animal figures; and c. the numerals, which marked the culmination in ascertaining their qualities and places of utterance.

Some of the texts, when read, appeared to reflect in the worn-out and decayed vocables of the RV:

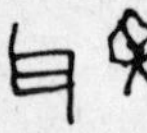 ṇa ga (the light has gone away)

: nág (night) RV 7,71,1.

 ṣa ṭha (the ball rolled)

 : sát (the rolling ball)

śa ma yo ṣa (let evil go, let comfort be there)

: śám yós (wellbeing welfare)

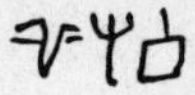 va ṇa ṣa (from the water the life comes)

: vánas in vanas-pati (plant)

ha ṭha ṣa (from the empty space a ball emerged)

: satás in sató-vīra,-bṛhat

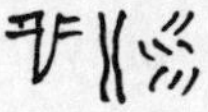 ṣa ra ṣa (from the nipple flows stops)

: sáras (pond, lake, sea).

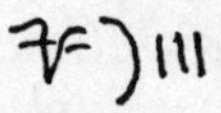 ta na śa (from the womb gems come out)

: tánas (offspring) 5,70,4.

Just a visual examination of the two sides suggested that the expanded forms of the Indus texts represent clauses which have been reduced to vocables in the RV. Even some theoretical reduction of the Indus clauses to the Vedic vocables and the expansion of the Vedic vocables to the Indus size produced surprising results. The language of the Indus inscriptions and Sanskrit fell in the straight line of genealogy.

There are three stages in the development of a language: isolating, agglutinative and inflexional. The Sanskrit language is inflexional, the Turkish or Swahili is agglutinative, and the modern Chinese is isolating. The graphic form of the language of the Indus texts suggested that it could not be inflexional. Because even loose affix elements are not visible, except some rare examples of a few sign-pairs, it could not be agglutinative too. It appeared to be isolating. Naturally, it may be supposed to be the grandmother of the Vedic language, two generations apart, the mother-stage of the Vedic language missing.

In two-sign texts, the first could be the subject and the second the verb. In three-sign texts, the natural order could be subject + object + verb, though, more naturally, it was generally the oblique case + subject + verb.

The Indus texts, interpreted in this light, gave interesting results. The Vedic vocables and the Indus clauses do not only agree phonetically but also semantically. Many nestors of the Vedic words are not derivable from the Vedic roots. They are the contracted forms of the Indus clauses. The words like sát, satás, etc. had blurred the vision not only of Roth, the founder of the Vedic philology, but even of Macdonell and Geldner. The Vedic words have not come from Central Asia but from the ruins of the Indus valley civilisation.

The language of the Indus texts follows certain principles of the linguistic embryology. A Vedic ṛṣi describes the growth of the grass in the following way: growing from stem to stem, from one knot to another .... (Vs 13,20). The language too grows in a similar way: s + v, s + o + v, oblique case + s + v, and so on. This is the first stage of the development of a language, called isolating. The clause contracts to form a phrase with the same body of syllables. Ultimately, it becomes a lexeme. By this time, the language gradually comes to the agglutinative stage. There was a clause gā va (goes into the stable). Later, it became a phrase gāva (going into the stable). Even as a lexeme, it is gāva (cattle) and its feminine from gāvī was known to Patañjali in the popular language. At the agglutinative stage, its plural form was gāva-ṣa. As this form reached the inflexional stage, the accent on the first syllable reduced it to gāvas, when it was analysed as gāv-as, giving birth to a new base gāu. Its later history is well-known. We can imagine, how its reconstructed IE form is a hoax.

It is this linguistic Darwinism which can lead us from the fossilised Vedic language to its primitive form, fortunately preserved in the Indus inscriptions. But it is bound to have far reaching consequences. The big giant called IE will have its natural death, or it will have to be killed. Then the milestones of history and archaeology will have to be crushed and the time-limits will have to be pushed further back by milleniums. The reckless dating of Hittite (1600 BC), Greek (1400 BC) and Vedic (1200 BC) will have to be drastically revised. Putting all phases of the Indus valley civilisation between 3500 BC and 1800 BC is an academic crime. The astronomical references are more reliable than the carbon-dating.

2

The Indus Language at the Grassroot of the Indian Society

In India, we have several languages, distinguished provincially and regionally with different names. We tend to think that India is not only polyglot but also multi-racial. Though the DNA test has proved that there is a single race from north to south, regarding language we still hold the view that certain groups of languages are genetically different from one another.

But as we go deep into the countryside and speak to the rustic and uneducated villagers, we find that they speak a language not known to us by name. We understand what they say, but as we analyse their language, we see that essentially it is not our own, because their language does not have any grammar worthy of name. When they begin to talk among themselves, we fail to understand what they say. It is here that we find that they speak a different language.

Anybody from any corner of India may have the same experience. He may talk to the rustic and uneducated villagers of his region and know that they speak a language different from his own. That is why, when they converse among themselves, they become unintelligible. We do not imagine any language now which is free from grammar, but there are languages without grammar even at present. If these rustic villagers from all corners of the countryside of India are brought together and left to converse among themselves, after some moments of unintelligibility, they will begin speaking a common language. It is not an experience, but a presumption.

As regards ourselves, we cannot devise a common language, because every group among us speaks a language having some amount of grammar. But what they speak is the grassroot language of the Indian society and perhaps as old as the early stage of agglutinative Indus itself. It was perhaps the stage of their language when the Indus communities had disintegrated. This language of the grassroot society did not ever die but remained under the feet of the dominating language of the region.

It came to surface in the 3rd century BC, when the emperor Aśoka engraved his inscriptions in the Volkssprache. We have been calling it 'old Prakrit', but essentially it is not Prakrit as it is understood by us. After Aśoka it went underground again and came under the feet of the dominating provincial and regional languages.

When, after the Muslim invasions on India, the provincial and regional languages became contaminated and a creole called Urdu evolved, the Hindu saints again turned to the grassroot language, which was known to the wandering saints. It was widely understood but hardly spoken anywhere, except at the grassroot of the society. That is why, the language of the Rām carit mānas of Tulsidās is understood far and wide in the country. It is said to be an old Awadhi, but this term is as vague as the 'old Prakrit'. That language has again gone underground.

We cannot say that the language of the Aśokan inscriptions or that of the Rām carit mānas has no grammar. Essentially the language is grammarless, but under pressure from the language of the upper level of the society, it was bound to distinguish cases and tenses and moods. Thus the language of the Aśokan inscriptions show association by -te, possession by -sa, location by -si, and so on. Even the Rām carit mānas is forced to use such tricks to avoid confusion. As a rule, it discards as much grammar as possible. A grammarless language is free from variation or has no dialects.

This long introduction is a prelude to a very controversial truth. I have been able to read a part of the Indus texts and, as such, I have come to know about the structure of the Indus language. At the initial stage of the language, there was no grammar. Therefore, there was no dialectal variation. Only the order of words showed the grammatical functions. The first place was allotted to the subject and the last to the verb. The oblique case pushed the subject to the second position and the object took position between subject and verb. Later, there were various manipulations in their order:

s + v: ṇa ga (light movement) = The light has gone away.

s + o + v: va ṇa ṣa (water life embryo) = The water gives life

obl. + s + v: ta na ṣa (womb gem embryo) = From womb gems come.

v + obl.: gā va (movement dwelling) = Goes into the pen. etc.

It was the isolating stage of the language.

A study of the texts further reveals that by the time of the writing of the inscriptions, it had already transited into the agglutinative stage. The following affix elements had developed;

(1) -gha for future

(2) -ga for order

dra-gha, ra-ga (conflagration-future, speed-order) seems to say: There will be a catastrophic fire; do run away.

(3) -ṭha for the past tense

ṣa-ṭha (be-past) = there was, contracted as ṣ-ṭha and physically lifted by the RV 7,103,9c

(4) -ra for pluperfect

ca-ra (be-pluperfect) = had been, had taken place; adopted by the RV in ku-cara (meaning doubtful) and go-cara (visible). Even Pāṇini noted it in bhūta-pūrva sense.

(5) -ha for perfect

ma-ha (time-perfect) = has grown old; it makes a clause tata maha (the father has grown old), contracted as tatā-maha ('grandfather), its -maha conceived as suffix in pitā-maha, etc.

(6) There was also a prefix ā- for the past tense, continuing in the Vedic form ā-ha (past-say) = said, ā-ṣa (past-be) = it was. Of these two verbal forms, āha was reduced to āḥ (an expression of grief) and āsa to āḥ (RV 10,129,3). Though āha continued with just five forms in Sanskrit, ās was extended by the Vedic endings to distinguish number and person: ās-am, ās-va, ās-an, etc.

At this very stage, when they had reached a considerable height in urbanisation and technical advancement, there was some tragic event: earth-quake, flood, conflagration, and all. On account of it, just with this meagre wealth of affix elements the communities had dispersed in different directions. Though the northern and western groups had established some sort of communication, the southern and eastern groups remained totally cut off from each other. As a matter of fact, the three groups did not know the fate of one another. Consequently, three linguistic groups emerged in India which, though evolving from the same common parents, did not know one another. They are now known as Aryan (northern), Dravidian (Southern) and Munda (central) languages, with their respective numerous dialects.

Under the favourable conditions of the nature, the Aryan language flowered extensively and abundantly at the agglutinative stage and, with the exuberant wealth of morphology, reached the inflexional stage. From its dizzy height there was a climb down and the beginning of the literary activities. They began composing hymns, sometimes singing the past glory of the lost urban civilization and sometimes glorifying the nature of the new surroundings. The officials of the lost urban civilization, Agni, Indra, Viṣṇu, Rudra, etc., became their gods and their real history became the Vedic mythology.

The inflexional Vedic language went on climbing down. After several milleniums, the inflexion disappeared and by the beginning of the second millenium, the analytic modern Indic emerged. It represented almost the same stage of the language at which it had originated. But while at the time of its origin the words were monosyllabic, of the CV or CCV type, at this stage there were words of VC, CV and CVC type with some amount of inflexion borrowed from the inflexional ancestor.

At the same period, it came in contact with the Persian language and a creolisation started in the language. The several dialects attained the status of the fully grown up languages and by the time of their coming into writing they had transited into the second round of the agglutinative stage, slightly different from that of the first round. These languages are isolating, agglutinative and inflexional at the same time, because they have also borrowed some amount of inflexion from the ancestor.

The southern and eastern branches of the Indus language developed independently in their own way at the agglutinative stage. The affix elements which were carried from the parent language became mixed with the new elements which developed independently in the respective languages, and their homogeneity was lost.

Just as gha for future, continuing till the RV, has been deaspirated to gā in the Hindi kar-e-gā, in Munda it is never used at the end. But ka seems to appear as suffix with a verb in the imperative sense. Perhaps it is the devoiced form of ga for 'order' in Indus. The prefix ā- for the past tense was shortened to a- already at the agglutinative stage, though ā has continued down to the Vedic language. But in Munda dialects this a- has continued to exist: a-ka-ta (he did, has done). This Munda-Santhal form suggests that person had begun to be distinguished at the time of disintegration.

In specific dialects in the countryside, there are some curious elements:

An affix ha is added to verbal forms to express a present perfect ('I have gone') idea, and only the 3rd person is distinguished, the first and second person remaining identical.

Similarly, an affix ra is added to a verbal form to express a pluperfect ('I had gone') idea.

It is surprising that these elements, making the perfect form ma-ha and the pluperfect form ca-ra had given the secondary suffixes -maha and -cara to Sanskrit, already noted by Pāṇini, are surviving even today in their seed-form.

Sri Aravinda has said: It is the retention of the common form and not their disappearance that is the miracle of the language.

Many of the secondary suffixes, coming down from the agglutinative Indus, noted by Pāṇini, are already obsolete in Sanskrit:

Though -cara (P.5,3,53) survives, -kuṇa and -jāha (5,2,24) as well as -cuñcu and -caṇa (5,2,26) are only restricted to the grammar. Even -kaṭa (5,2,29) and -kuṭāra (5, 2, 30) were disappearing from the language, when Pāṇini arrested them. Though -biḍa (flat nose) is treated as a suffix, it is itself a base in biḍ-āla (flat-nosed = cat). The agglutinative Indus forms, cipiṭa, cikina (flat-nosed), used even today, were explained by Pāṇini with the Sanskrit material.

It is difficult to say whether the writers of Kāśikā really knew the meaning of those obsolete words or they have just quoted from some ancient sources, and the commentaries on them have hardly tried to clarify them.

Really, Pāṇini is not as young as we know him to be, and also not merely concerned with his bhāṣā alone. He knew even the oldest ancestor of ur-Sanskrit in its original script, though he did not employ it in his teaching of the Sanskrit grammar, because the inflexional Sanskrit could not be graphed in the outdated script.

As we talk to the villagers in the countryside, specially to those who are without any modern education, we hear such words and expressions which do not belong to the modern society.

While quoting somebody verbatim, without naming him, one says; kī do = what they say ('is that). A collection of such words and phrases will lead us back to that community who uttered them.

While calling our domestic dog for a morsel of food in the countryside, we speak an Indus clause of the isolating stage; a tū ā = O dog, come.

What we call incense-burner or manger about the field-symbol in the Indus script is even now to be seen in the countryside, called nādī, and the grass put therein is called sānī. Our domestic cat is called billī (= biḍa-lī 'flat-nosed'), and a wild cat is called biḍāla bilār (flat-nosed). The house-rat is called cūhā (speaking gently). A complete silence is called cū.

It is not the work of a single researcher to collect all such expressions, which are the immortal words of the bygone age. The collections of such expressions will reveal some common vocabulary of the Indian languages, which will show the common parentage of all the Indian languages and a homogenous race at the grassroot of the society. The idea is likely to be ridiculed, but it is the only truth.

3

The Indus Inscriptions do Speak Now

Unable to describe the charmingness of Rāma and Lakṣmaṇa, an innocent friend of Sītā said to her: how should I describe the dark and white princes ?, my speech has no eyes and my eyes have no speech.

Similar was the fate of the prevedic, the socalled Indus culture. But now the inscriptions have begun to speak and we may be able to have the first hand account of the Indus culture.

The Indus inscriptions have come down to us in three scripts: the animal figures, the geometrical figures and the numerals. The numerals of the specific length and shape in the strict order from right to left are represented by the syllabic order of the Māheśvarasūtras at the beginning of the Pāṇini's grammar. In the duplicate and triplicate texts, they indicate the phonemic values of the geometrical and animal figures. Thus the following is the Indus syllabary in three scripts in the syllabic order of the Māheśvarasūtras:

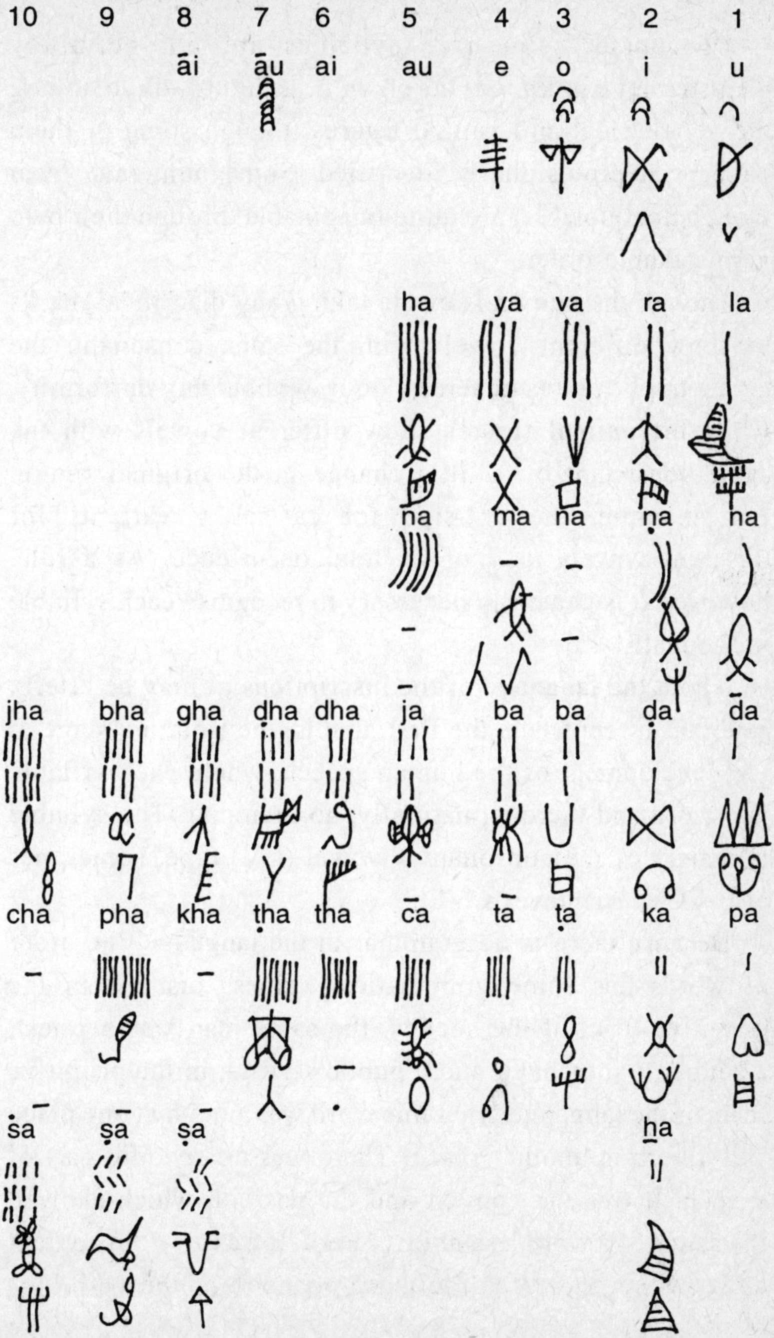

10 9 8 7 6 5 4 3 2 1
āi āu ai au e o i u
ha ya va ra la
na ma na ṇa na
jha bha gha ḍha dha ja ba ba ḍa d̄a
cha pha kha ṭha tha c̄a t̄a ṭa ka pa
ṡa ṣa ṣa h̲a

Of course, some rare syllables are not definitely identifiable; e.g. kh, ch, th, ph, ṅ, ñ, j, jh, ṭ, ḍ, ḍh, b among the geometrical and animal figures, though some of them have been provisionally identified. Some numerals, even though not quotable, are quite imaginable through their own unmistakable order.

Though the numerals evade taking any diacritical marks to show different vowels with the same consonant, the geometrical figures generally do it, without any uniformity, while the animal figures show different vowels with the same consonant by a little change in the original figure. For example, the ant-sign for ca has 6 variants for different vowels in 7 of its total occurrence. As a rule, however, it is generally necessary to recognise each syllable individually.

About the language of the inscriptions, it may be briefly said that it represents the first, that is, the isolating stage in the development of the human speech, where each syllable is a word and there is, naturally, no grammar. The syllable is mainly of the consonant + vowel (CV) type, sometimes also CCV, but never CVC.

Because there is no grammar in the language, the order of words has some grammatical values. Just as, in the primitive form of the society, the same man was a priest, a soldier, a merchant, and a public servant, in the primitive form of the language, the same word was a noun at one place and a verb at another place. There was no specific part of speech. It was the context and the position which showed the status of a word as a noun or verb. It was also the context alone which indicated the tense or mood of the verb.

In two-syllable texts, the first is the subject and the second is the verb; ṇa ga 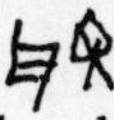(light movement) means: the light has gone away (= the darkness has come). In three-syllable texts, the order is either subject + object + verb: va ṇa ṣa 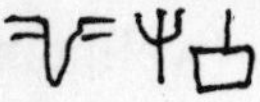 (water life embryo) meaning 'the water gives life', or oblique-case + subject + verb : ta na ṣa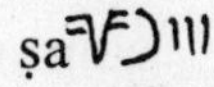  (womb gem embryo) meaning 'from the womb gems come out'. In the later phase of the language, at the isolating stage itself, perhaps not or rarely represented in the inscriptions, this original order was variously changed for specific purposes; e.g. there was also verb + oblique case : gā va (goes into the pen); oblique case + verb : bī ja (in the water it grows); subject + compound verb : a mba (she gives-milk), and so on. Perhaps the vowels referred to the nameless objects, which later became pronouns, and the consonants were for the nouns and verbs.

With this breakdown of the language, let us see the following texts:

The clause ṇa ga has contracted as nag (night), occurring only once in the RV (7,71,1).

The clause ṣa ṭha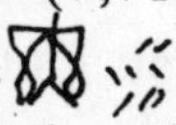 (embryo circle) means: the egg rolled forth, and it has been reparaphrased in the RV (10,121,1): hiraṇya-garbhaḥ sam-avartatāgre (a golden egg rolled forth in the beginning). The clause itself was phonetically reduced as sát in the RV, but the original meaning 'the rolling egg' was somehow confused with the homonym sát, the present participle from as 'to be'. Thus this word was misunderstood from the very beginning of its creation, and neither Sāyaṇa nor Ġeldner could understand it properly. Though the seers of the Upaniṣads had some idea of the 'rolling egg', the commentators did not pick up the point.

The text śa ma yo ṣa 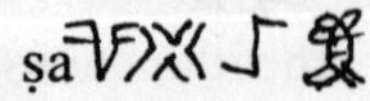 (evil end comfort embryo) means: let evil end, let comfort be there. These are two clauses. They contracted as śám yós (wellbeing and comfort) in the RV. While śam continued in the compounds like śaṅ-kara, śam-bhu, etc., yós disappeared after the RV.

The clause va ṇa ṣa contracted as vánas in vanas-pati (plant). It was reduced further to varṣ (vṛṣ) 'to rain' in the Vedic language itself, which has a number of derivatives.

The text ta na ṣa has contracted as tánas (offspring), occurring only once in the RV (5,70,4).

From tánas, the verb tan (to expand) was deduced, because the family expands through the offsprings. It is an IE verb. This tan, through its various forms (tan-o-ti, *tan-a-ti, *tan-ā-ti), has given birth to tan-class, su-class (su-no-ti), rudh-class (ru-ṇa-ddhi) and krī-class (krī-ṇā-ti) in the Vedic grammar. The old vocable tánas was further reduced to tarṣ 'to be thirsty', because the desire for a son is a kind of thirst, and this thirst had reached even the Germanic people (Gothic Thars, Eng. thirst, German Durst).

The text h̲a ṭha ṣa 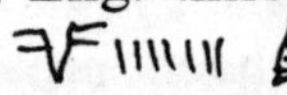 (empty-space disc embryo) means 'from the empty space a ball emerged'. This clause contracted as satás in sató-vīra, -mahat, -bṛhat, but this satás is clear neither to Sāyaṇa nor to Geldner, etc.

The text h̲a ḍha ṣa 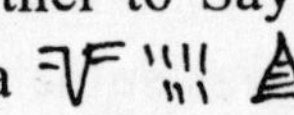 (empty-space sound embryo) means; in the empty space there was a big bang. It has contracted as sadha (heaven) in sadha-stha (staying in the heaven) and -mād (rejoicing in the heaven), which is wrongly associated with saha (with), the particle.

The text la ṭha 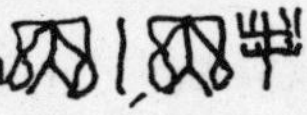 (time circle) means: the time turns round, and has contracted as ṛtá (the regular order of the universe) in the RV. Another possible text la ṭhu with almost the same meaning appears in Avesta as ratu (time) corresponding to the Vedic ṛtú (season).

The text ma ṇa 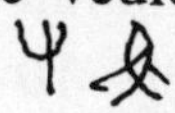 probably means 'the moon shines', and it seems to have contracted as mán in the RV (8,78,2), which probably means 'ornament', shining like the moon.

The words of this type, namely mán above, rán from ra ṇa ṣa, rám from ra ma (the fire is extinguished, turns into ash), etc. have not even been entered in the Vedic dictionaries, because they are not derivable from the Vedic roots. Though rám-su has been analysed in the pada-pāṭha, rám (ash) has been left out by Roth and it has been wrongly understood by Geldner. The word rāma 'a black man' cannot be derived form the root *ram,* because it comes from the Indus source. The arrogance of the western scholarship in ignoring even the analysis of the pada text of the RV is very painful.

The text ṣa ra ṣa 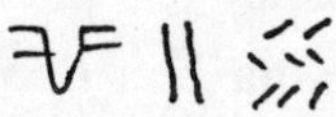 (nipple speed end) means: from the mountain flows (and) stops (at the sea). It was contracted as sáras (pond, lake, sea), and it is the base of the river which later came to be called Saras-vat-ī (abounding in lakes or ponds).

By this clause, we can imagine the date of these inscriptions. It was a time at the isolating stage of the language, when an object was indicated through its action, because the 'naming' was a later event. Though the same river was there at the time of the writing of the inscriptions, it was indicated through a clause. We can imagine the time taken in a clause changing into a phrase (flowing from the mountain and stopping at the sea) and then into a lexeme (a pond, lake or sea), further the same sáras taking the possessive suffix -vat and the feminine suffix -ī. It could push the writing of the inscriptions 10 thousand years or more back. The starting of the academic activities by the writing of the hymns on the bank of Sarasvatī may be pushed back accordingly.

The syllable na itself means 'it flows'. It was extended by another syllable da 'makes noise', and thus na-da means 'flows and makes indistinct noise'. From this nada or f. nad-ī the verb nad was deduced meaning 'avyakte śabde'.

In this respect, sindhu is a river of comparatively recent origin, because it is derived from syand 'to go, roll' according to Yāska. The centre of that prevedic civilisation was naturally the river Sarasvatī.

To be very brief, some peculiar vedic vocables can be seen in the Indus inscriptions:

sabda 'bright'	:	h̲a bha dha (in the sky light burns)
rāma 'a black man'	:	rā rā rā ma (fires are extinguished)
tata 'father'	:	ta ṭha (the womb turns)
ṛcīṣa 'frying pan'	:	ra cī ṣa (the fire causes heat)
riśā-das 'well-wisher'	:	-da ṣa (speak wisely)
		etc.

While the inscriptions were being written, the language too was becoming more expressive. Therefore, before the emergence of the affix elements, a trick was developed to connect two clauses. Either to show 'if-then' relationship between two clauses, or just to express some subjunctive idea, or to express the conjunction 'because', the verb of the first clause was bent towards u:

ga ṣu va ṇa ṣa 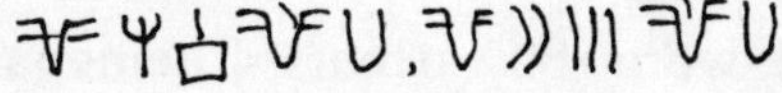

(plant embryo water life embryo)

= The plants may grow, the water gives life.
the plant grows, because the water gives life.
if the water gives life, the plant grows.

Another form of these clauses is seen even now in the rustic compound gāchh-brichh (plants in general)

The second part of the text va ṇa ṣa ṇā ṣa has fossilised as -nās in the controversial anās, which is wrongly interpreted as nose-less (a-nās) or face-less (an-ās), based on the racial interpretation of the RV, being the physical features of Dāsa and Dasyu, who are taken to be non-Aryans. As a matter of fact, they were the dwellers of the mountainous villages, but were 'unwise and ignorant' because of lack of education. The clause ṇā ṣa means 'know' (and) 'see', and the fossilised form nās meant 'wisdom and knowledge', so that a-nās began to express 'unwise and ignorant'. A number of words in the RV of very good intention have been similarly guillotined by the racial interpretation.

There is an important text showing the urban culture of the Indus people. The text bu jña ṣu ḍho ṣa 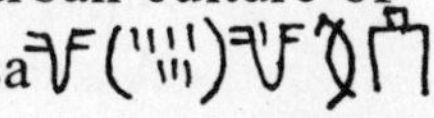 says: if the water is contaminated, siphon it out, The second part of the text now stands for ḍhos, the siphoning instrument in the countryside.

Another text ra bī ṣu va ṇa ṭha (fire water heat, dwelling vapour disc) says : if the fire heats the water, in the dwelling the vapour circulates. The first part of the text has contracted as ṛbīsa 'a cavity in the earth from which hot vapours arise' and the second has contracted as vanád 'fire'.

The word ṛbīsa occurs 4 items in the RV, and everytime it describes the horrifying experiences of the Atris, who were rescued by Aśvins.

This incident does not relate to the RV but to the citizens of the Indus culture, where the Atris were the men of the fire-brigade and Aśvins were the men of the rapid action force. When the urban culture collapsed, the men of the fire-brigade became the fire-priests and the men of the rapid action force became the physicians of the gods.

The vocable vanád of the second part occurs only once in the RV, and Grasmann has very ingeniously derived it from van-ad (consuming the wood). We can see how the same meaning may come from different sources.

While the inscriptions were going on being written, the language was gradually transiting in to the next, that is, the agglutinative stage.

At least two affix elements are seen in large number: gha for future and ga for order, and it is also interesting to note that all occurrences of gha are followed by ga:

dra-gha, ra-ga 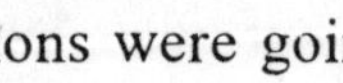
(conflagration-future, speed-order)
= A catastrophic fire will take place; do run away

na pra gha, va ga 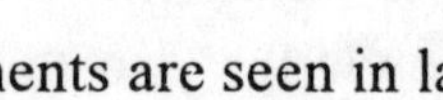
(unbroken storm-future, arm-order)
= A continuous storm will start; do take care;

Perhaps, dra-gha has fossilised as drāk (immediately), and pra-gha as prāk (in the east).

ha ṭha, ra ga 
(sky circle, speed-order)
= An avalanche rolls hither; run away
ha ṭha-gha, va-ga 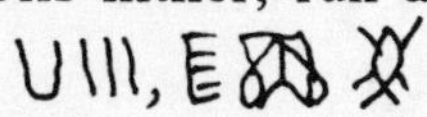
(sky circle-future, arm-order)
= An avalanche will roll hither, do take care.

These texts may remind us of the events of the glacial ages, when villages after villages were washed away by avalanches.

There are also texts which may be interpreted as small inscriptions of the veterinary hospitals, some others of the maternity hospitals.

There are instances of other affix elements, but they are, more or less, doubtful. However, it may be pointed out that the following affix elements too gradually developed in the language.

There was the prefix ā- for the past tense, still continuing in āsa (there was) from ā-ṣa (past be) and āha (said) from ā-ha (past-say). Of them, āsa was reduced to ās (āḥ) in the RV (10,129, 3b) and again expanded as ās-am, ās-an, etc. and āha was reduced to āḥ (an expression of grief), but it was retained with just five forms.

The affix -ha for perfect attached to ma (to grow old) made a clause tata maha (the father has grown old) at the agglutinative stage, which was contracted as tatā-maha (grandfather) at the Vedic stage, analogically giving birth to words like pitā-maha, etc.

The suffix-ra for pluperfect was attached to ca (to be, take place), the form cara appearing in the contracted words kucara and gocara, later appearing as a secondary suffix in the sense of bhūta-pūrva.

Much more was there at the agglutinative stage of the Indus language to justify the wealth of morphology of the Vedic language.

The Indus inscriptions are not dumb now.

4

From Language to Culture

Taking note of the conflicting or, at least, indecisive evidences of the archaeology and related disciplines, scholars have now pinned their hopes on the decipherment of the Indus script for determining the exact ethnological status of the Vedic people. If the language of the Indus inscriptions is proved to be related with the language of RV, nobody can deny the identity of the Indus and Vedic cultures.

The archaeology has been the main tool in showing the precedence of one culture to another.But the overlapping of the two cultures cannot be easily decided. That is why, the Indus culture after its nature phase and Vedic culture in its early phase is said be synchronous, taking for granted that the former precedes the latter.

If the linguistic evidence comes to support the archaeology, the result may be more decisive. However, though the carbon-dating is employed in archaeology to determine the period approximately, the language does not come under its sphere of investigation. For dating the linguistic evidences, some other tools have to be employed.

The astronomy seems to have the same relevance with respect to language and literature as the carbon-dating has with archaeology.Thus, if the astronomical references agree with carbon-dating, we may reach some point of agreement with regard to time. If the evidence of an historical language is put forward, there cannot be any doubt about the veracity of the period. But the evidence of a reconstructed language cannot be accepted. And the whole structure of the IE language is hypothetical.

If we have to take resort to IE, we will have to change our modus operandi regarding the linguistic reconstruction. So far, we have been putting a blanket over the cognate forms to show the parent form. For example, for Sansk. pitár, Gk, Latin, patēr, etc.we have been reconstructing IE *pater; for Sansk, áśva, Av. aspa, Latin equus, Gk hippos, Eng. Horse, etc., we have reconstructed *ekwos. Sri Arvinda (The secret of the Veda. The Origins of The Aryans speech, pp.551-581) criticised this mode of reconstruction, because the language does not orginate in that way.

Just as a plant grows, from stem to stem, from knot to knot, the language too grows syllable by syllable. In this connection, we may bring the controversial 'horse' which is said to be non-existent in the Indus valley. Following some kind of linguistic embryology, we can say that the horse was native to the Indus civilisation.

If the Sanskrit lexicons of the monosyllabic words have any authority in respect of their preserving the monosyllabic words of the ancestral language, ha for 'horse' attests the existence of horses in the Indus valley, at least in its most primitive breed.Of the two sounds, the voiced ha and the voiceless ha of the Indus syllabary, as represented by the syllabic order of the Máhśvarasūtras, it is the voiceless ha for 'horse'. This ha was extended in Vedic by -śa for 'injury' and -va for 'strength'. Thus *ha-śva was a horse which was 'injurious' (through its hind-leg) and 'strong'. It evolved later as a-ś-va (losing the voiceless ha). Its Iranian breed was extended by -śa-pha '(injurious) hoof' and *ha-ś-pha evolved as a-spa (also losing the voiceless h) in Av. Its Roman breed was extended by -kva, and there is equus in Latin.

Its Greek breed was extended by -pva, and hippos retains the original h in Gk. In Germanic it was extended by -rsa, and from the Germanic -hors (retaining the original h), we have 'horse' in English. The base ha- was extended by -ra (speed) and va (strength) in Vedic, so that *ha-r-va apears as arvā (arvan) in Vedic, perhaps another breed of the horse. This *ha-r-va was added to gand- (which is the same base as garda- in garda-bha 'ass') and gandharva is again a new breed of the horse, an assed horse, perhaps a 'donkey'. Thus formation of the cognate words for a 'horse' does not only show its root in the original language, but also its place of birth in India.

We have come from the root of the word to its final form. Let us go in opposite direction and see how the reconstructed IE is fallacious and non-existent. In the plural form gāvas, we are inclined to see the agglutinative form *gāva-ṣa form the base gāva- (because the feminine gāvī was known to Patañjali), the final vowel lost due to accent on the first syllable. The base gāva- itself was a phrase ('going into stable') some time ago, whch has evolved from the clause gā va (goes into the stable) at the isolating stage of the language. Here also we see, how a form grows like a plant: the clause gā va (goes into the stable), the phrase gāva (going inside the stable), the lexeme gāva (bull), pl. gāva-ṣa, Vedic gāvas, later analysed as gāu + as, giving birth to the Vedic stems: gāu- in strong forms, gau- in weak forms before vowels, and go- before consonants. Thus the reconstructed IE *g-ou- is non-existent.

Let us now proceed forward with ṇa ra meaning 'a creature goes'. This is the isolating stage of the language.

At the agglutinative stage, it contracts as a phrase with the same body of syllables; ṇara (a moving creature). It also turns up as a lexeme (a man, an animal, a creature), and its pl. form is ṇara-ṣa. At the inflexional stage, it is reduced to náras due to accent on the first syllable. This pl. form was analysed in Vedic as nar-as, and the base nṛ- emerged. We see that a word is formed syllable by syllable, and the reconstruction of the whole body of an historical word is an erroneous procedure. Thus the whole castle of the IE language has to be demolished. This demolition was already predicted indirectly by Hirt, who said: It really does not matter what was spoken in IE; what matters are the ablaut relationships.

Let us see how the texts of the Indus inscriptions read in the manner of an isolating language are seen transiting into the Vedic language:

Indus texts

1. ṇa ga (light movement) = the light has gone away (the darkness has come).
2. ṣa ṭha (embryo circle) = the ball rolled.
3. ta na ṣa (womb gem embryo) = from the womb gems come out.
4. śa ma yo ṣa (evil end comfort embryo) = let evil end; let comfort be there.
5. va ṇa ṣa (water life embryo) = from the water life comes.
6. rau ci ṣa (fire light embryo) = from the fire the light comes.
7. na bha ṣa (sky light embryo) = in the sky there is light.
8. va ṇa ra (dwelling creature speed) = in the dwelling the creatures go.

9. va ṭha ṣa (dwelling disc embryo) = from the womb foetus comes out.
10. ha ṭha ṣa (empty space disc embryo) = from the empty space a ball emerged.
11. ha ḍha ṣa (empty space sound embryo) = in the empty space there was a big bang.
12. la ṭha (time circle) = the time turns round.
13. ṣa ra ṣa (nipple speed end) = flows from the mountain and stops on the way.
14. ra bī ṣu va ṇa ṭha (fire water heat dwelling vapour circle) = if the fire heats the water, in the dwelling the vapour circulates.

Vedic vocables (number-wise)

1. nág (night) RV.
2. sát (the rolling ball), later confused with the participal sát 'existing', also paraphrased: hiraṇya-garbhaḥ samavartatāgre RV.
3. tánas (offspring) RV 5,70,4
4. śám yós (wellbeing and comfort)
5. vánas in vanas-pati (plant)
6. rócis (light)
7. nábhas (sky)
8. vanar- in vanar-gu, -ṣád cf. vānar-a 'monkey'
9. vatsá (calf)
10. satás in sató-vīra, -mahat -bṛhat
11. sadha (heaven)
12. ṛtá (the order of the universe), cf. ṛtú Av. ratu
13. sáras (pond, lake, sea) in sarasvatī
14. ṛbīsa (a cavity in the earth from which hot vapours come) vanád (fire)

There are many other texts which too may be shown to

have transited into the Vedic vocables, but they require a good deal of phonetic exercise. It is not a proper place for them.

Thus it is linguistically proved that the Vedic language is in the genealogical line of the language of the Indus inscriptions. Then it is autmoatically proved that the Vedic culture is the continuation of the Indus culture and is correspondingly predated by the culture represented by the language of the Indus inscriptions.That is to say, there is continuity in the Indus and Vedic culture as proved by the continuity of the language.

But there is also a break in the contunity of the language. The extant record of the Indus inscriptions shows that the language had just entered the agglutinative stage, and except gha for future, ga for order, ra for pluperfect and ṭha for past, there is no trace of the other affix elements, which are so extensively and abundantly represented in the Vedic language. It is true that a large number of them would have developed at the spring time of the Vedic language.The meagre examples of the language of the inscriptions,however, make us imagine that there was a tragic disintegration of the Indus community at the very beginning of the agglutinative stage of their language.

It may be presumed that the communities under the favourable conditions of the nature carried their language to the inflexional stage, but those who faced hard conditions just limped with their language at the agglutinative stage. It is justified to assume that they disintegrated in four groups: the southern group went to the extreme south in the land of the hot sun, dra-vi-ḍa or dra-mi-ḍa as they called it; the eastern group went to the hills and forests of the central India; the western group went to the land of the Soma plants on the Iran-Afghan border; and the northern group settled on the land watered by the seven rivers, not far away from the devastated region. While the northern and western groups remained in touch with each other, the southern and eastern groups remained cut off. Therefore, though the language of the northern and western groups did not deviate very much from each other, apart from some regional variations as apparent from the linguistic styles of the languages of the RV and that of the other saṃhitās and Brāhamas. The languages of the eastern and southern groups gradually became exotic to each other. They also remained limping at the agglutinative stage and developed in their own way throughout their history upto the present day.

The language of the northern and western groups reached the inflexional stage, though at the grassroot of the society a form of the agglutinative Indus pervaded the whole country, a later form of which appears in the language of the Aśokan inscriptions and a still later form of which appears in the Rām-carit-mānas of Tulsidās. We do not know how far the northern group proceeded to further north, but the western group had open vista before them and proceeded towards western Asia on their way to Europe. They stayed for quite a long time in West India, because the Hittite language has preserved both the voiceless and voiced h, which were not only normalised as the voiced h in Vedic but its voiceless pronunciation was declared to be a fault.

Just as the agglutinative stage of the Indus language is gloriously absent between the Indus inscriptions and the Vedic literature, the archaeology too is dumbly silent between the Indus and Vedic culture.

The ruins of the agglutinative stage of Indus, however, can be assembled from the vast field of the Vedic literature:

1. The Vedic clause iti has āsa (thus indeed it was) is the naturalised version of the agglutinative Indus clause i-ti ha ā-ṣa (this-manner, say, past-be) = thus, they say, it was.
2. The Indus agglutinative form ā-ṣa (past-be) was reduced to ās (=āḥ) in the RV (10,129,3 b) : apraketaṃ sarvaṃ salilam ā idam (indistinguishable all it was water).
3. The Indus agglutinative form ṣa-ṭha (be-past) was contracted as ṣ-ṭha and is attested in the RV (7,103,7c) : samvatsarasya tad ahaḥ pari ṣṭha = On that day of the year (you) around be-past = have surrounded (the pond).
4. The word náras in the RV (7,103,9b) is truly inflexonal, but in meaning it limps near the agglutinative stage and means 'creature',not netāras (Sāyaṇa) or men (Macdonell) or Herren (Geldner).
5. The secondary suffix -cara of Pāṇini is the pluperfect form ca-ra (had been, had taken place) of the agglutinative Indus, which was abscure even to the editors of the pada-pāṭha who do not analyse kucara (RV 1,154,2). The same later appears in gocara (visible).
6. The perfect form ma-ha (time-perfect = has grown old) seems to have made a clause tata maha (the father has grown old) in the agglutinative Indus, which had already contracted as tatā-maha in the RV, and it became a model for pitā-maha, etc.
7. There are several secondary suffixes of this type, noted by Pāṇini but hardly clear to his commentators.

If similar artefacts of the intermediate culture can be found, the Indus and Vedic culture can be linked archaeologically.

At this point, let us see how much help can be obtained

from astronomy. A stanza of the RV 7,103,9 runs thus:

devá-hitim jugupur dvādaśásya
ṛtum náro ná prá minanty eté,
saṃvatsaré prāvṛṣy āgatāyām
taptā gharmā aśnuvate visargám

"They have guarded the divine order; these creatures do not infringe time. In the year the rain having come, the warm sweat finds release."

If the numeral dvādaśa is accented on the first syllable, it is the cardinal 12. If it is accented on the last syllable, it is the ordinal 12th. An ordinal number also indicates the whole group, from 1 to 12, and also stands for the 'year', as rightly understood by Jakobi, who imagined that at this period of the RV the year began with the rainy season near the summer solstice.

It refers to the period when the sidereal sun was on the star śravaṇa at the coming autumnal equinox and, therefore, the year began with śrāvaṇa at the beginning of the rainy season. Even now the pañcāngas in Mithilā begin the year with śrāvaṇa. As we now consult the ephemeris, the sidereal sun has receded 126 deg. back and is on the star Uttarāphālgunī. Dividing this 126 by 50.3", the rate of precession per year, it refers to a period 9000 years from now. Thus, at least this stanza of the RV takes us back to 7000 BC.

Through some workable archaeological evidences we have been able to know that the Indus civilisation predates the Vedic, even though its last phase and the beginning of the Vedic civilisation may be synchronous. However, when the earliest phase of the Indus civilisation is restricted to 3500 BC, the astronomical evidence becomes weak.

The drying up of the mighty river Sarasvatī by 1900 BC

itself pushes the period of the RV several centuries back. Then the coming of the inflexional stage in Indus, which itself predates the mature stage of the Vedic language, would have been the result of several centuries. Thus 3500 BC cannot be the period of the beginning of the Indus civilisation. It must be pushed back to agree with the astronomical reference, because the astronomical evidence is not weaker than the archaeological.

The RV says that Sarasvatī was a mighty river. A text of the Indus inscriptions, 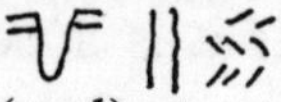 ṣa ra ṣa, seems to say: from the mountain flows (and) stops (at the sea). That is to say, the writer of the Indus inscriptions knows and sees the river flowing but does not name it. As a matter of fact, at the isolating stage of a language, an object could be indicated through its action. In other words, a river might be there, but it could be indicated as na (it flows). It is much later that the verb could become a noun, and then there was the formation of a clause by noun (subject) + verb. This phase of the isolating stage of the Indus language may go thousands of years before writing could have been introduced. Because the speakers of the language were the same people, the period may be pushed thousands of years back. Therefore, the period of 7000 BC should not be disbelieved. The fossilisation of the clause ṣa ra ṣa as sáras and then the formation of Sarasvatī may consume several thousand years.

Thus the archaeological and astronomical evidences can be adjusted with respect to time.

If linguistically it has been proved that the same amṛtasya putrāḥ (sons of immortals) have been inhabiting the entire region, we should start a fresh study of the archaeological, anthropological and linguistic material and come to some cogent conclusion.

5

The Dating of the Linguistic Material

At present, we in India speak a language which is at the agglutinative stage, to use an outdated term. It is otherwise in the analytic state, which is the he result of the dropping down of the morphological elements from the inflexional Apabhramśa, itself at the third station from the highly inflexional Sanskrit. Naturally, the modern north Indian languages are analytic: isolating, agglutinative and inflexional at the same time. This is not the case with the south Indian and Munda languages, which are marking time at the agglutinative stage for a long time. The plant of language, which branched in V-shape after the first knot of the isolating stage, could not have an identical development. Though the one arm of V reached the inflexional stage, the other crumbled down and remained limping at the agglutinative stage. The climb down from the last phase of the inflexional stage and coming to the present agglutinative stage in respect of the north Indian languages comprises hardly more than a thousand years.

But the inflexional stage of the Indian language, even through a conservative estimate, spreads over two thousand years (from 1000 BC to 1000 AD). The isolating Hindustani, of which there is no record left, become agglutinative before it came on record, because the contact with a foreign language expedited linguistic change. Otherwise, the native language is generally very slow towards change.

Let us mark the gradual simplification of the highly inflexional Vedic down to Apabhramśa. It is a story of the slow crumbling down of a citadel. The building of this citadel should have taken more time than its decay. The whole wealth of morphology inherited by the Vedic language from its agglutinative parents disappeared within two thousand years. Should the accumulation of this wealth be restricted to certain period ? It is impossible, or, at least, very difficult to ascertain. Even stating its destruction within two thousand years in untrue. It is hard to believe that the Sanskrit language is just as old as 1000 BC. We have no carbon-dating system for the linguistic change. The verb dekha-ti (sees) of the Aśokan inscriptions has hardly changed at its base even now. We can imagine the fate of a coin during this period.

Then let us start from the origin of the Aryan speech. Speaking linguistically, following an ironically nomenclatured "linguistic Darwinism", it should have been an isolating language, having monosyllabic words and no grammar. Each syllable or an articulated human sound, as distinguished from the clucking of the monkeys or the babbling of the cavemen, which would have preceded it, pointed to some physical object or living being, which was initially its activity, then its name. That is to say, initially ka pointed to the clucking of the peacock (: it clucks or produces a ka-sound), and then to the peacock itself (:it is a ka = peacock); the same ka pointed to some different varieties of beings and physical objects, avoiding all possible clashes of referends, so that the same ka referred to dozens of living beings or physical objects. Thus, gradually, ka was the noun peacock, the verb 'to cry' like a peacock, and the adjective 'speckled' like a peacock, and so on. This process may be carried on with respect to all syllables. Just as the same man in the primitive society was a priest, a warrior, a merchant and a public servant, the same syllable served as all parts of speech. From the evidence of the syllables in the Māheśvarasūtras, we may suppose that there were initially 33 consonants with 14 vowels, making 462 syllables, apart from various ligatures, theoretically amounting to more than 15000 monosyllabic words.

Now a stage came in the language for the making of a clause. The phase of a syllable standing for an activity (:na = it flows and na-da= it flows and makes an indistinct noise) was over. A verb used to follow a noun to make a clause: ṇa (a living being, a creature, an animal) ra (speed) made a clause ṇa ra (an animal goes). Hundreds or thousands of such clauses emerged. Later the clauses began to increase in length. First of all, an object began to separate the subject and the verb: ṇa ma ṣa (knowledge produces happiness). Then the oblique case made its appearance, which was placed at the first place, pushing the subject to the second position: ta na ṣa (From the womb gems come out). Even the verb used to begin a clause : gā va (Goes into the dwelling). Our Sanskrit grammarians had some faint idea about this phase of the ancient language, because when they said "gacchati iti gauḥ" (the cow is so called because it goes), they knew this gāva (and the feminine gāvī was also known to Patañjali). We are talking about the isolating stage of a language, and Patañjali knew a word of the slightly later stage. Can we imagine, how old this word gāvī may be?

So far, there is no reference to time in the language. Only the context showed whether it was a past or present. But the society had travelled a long distance. It had advanced culturally. The time had to be specified. It was carried out by prefixing ā- to a verb : ā-ṣa (past-be) = it was, there was; ā-ha (past-say) = said. They also needed a future-form and an order-form, and it was carried out by suffixing gha and ga respectively: dra gha, ra ga (conflagration-future, speed-order) = There will be a conflagration; please do run away.

With this idea in our mind, just conceived through the study of the Indus inscriptions themselves, let us turn to the Indus texts.

As we look at them, they are isolated syllables, also a group of two, three and more syllables. A group of two may represent s + v or v + oblique case or vice versa. A group of three may represent s + o + v or oblique case + s +v. The longer texts may contain so many similar clauses. There are a few clauses with the future affix gha, injunctive affix ga, and perhaps the past affix ṭha. The language of the inscriptions does not give any more information on morphology at this stage.

But some more morphological elements are imaginable from the records of the Vedic language : A verbal from ṣ-ṭha, itself a reduced from of the more original ṣa-ṭha (be-past) of the agglutinative stage occurs in the RV (7,103,9c):

> saṃvatsarasya tad ahaḥ pari ṣṭha = On that day of the year around be-past (you have surrounded the pond).

This agglutinative form definitely predates the usual Vedic form. What date can be assigned to it ?

We have a carbon-dating system to evaluate the age of coin or earthen pot. But do we have any such system to measure the time for the evolution of a form?

There is another verbal form ās (it was) in the RV (10,129,3b), which appears to belong to the inflexional stage, reduced from the agglutinative form ā-ṣa (past-be) due to accent, but predating the usual Vedic forms ās-am ās-ma, etc.; showing the distinction of number and person. The language of the RV does not attest these unusual forms of the border.

These forms of the border between the agglutinative and inflexional Indus have been used by the singers of the RV, because they were adjacent to them in time. Of course, āsa and āha have been used upto the last day of Sanskrit. Even the verb ha (to say) of the isolating Indus has continued in Sanskrit as almost meaningless particle. But they do not give any hint about their age.

A verbal form ma-ha (time-perfect = has grown old) of the agglutinative clause tata maha (the father has grown old), later contracted as tatā-maha (grandfather), has appeared as a suffix in Vedic pitā-maha, etc.; the pluperfect form ca-ra (be-pluperfect = had been, had taken place) of the agglutinative Indus, found in the contracted forms ku-cara, go-cara, has been noted as suffix by Pāṇini. But through them we cannot determine the age of the RV. They only show that the language of the RV goes farther back in the ruins of the Indus inscriptions.

It is true that the history of words cannot pinpoint the period of the evolution and change of the language. But there must be something to date the linguistic material. Corresponding to the carbon-dating for the archaeological objects, there are astronomical evidences for the life of a language.

The same Maṇḍūka-hymn (7,103) which has preserved the agglutinative Indus form ṣ-ṭha, also offers an astronomical evidence about the period of the composition of this hymn. It also suggests the period of the Vedic language.

When the numeral dvādaśa is accented on the first syllable, it is the cardinal number 12, but when it is accented on the last syllable, it is the ordinal 12th. Prof. Jakobi rightly understood dvādaśá as referring to 'year' and imagined that at this period of the RV the year began with the rainy season near the summer solstice.

It means that during this period the sidereal sun was on the star śravaṇa at the coming autumnal equinox and, therefore, the year began with śrāvaṇa at the beginning of the rainy season. Even now the pañcānga in Mithilā begins the year in śrāvaṇa.As we now consult the ephemeris, the sidereal sun has receded 126 deg. back and is on the star Uttarāphālgunī. Dividing this 126 with 503", the rate of precession per year, it refers to a period 9000 years from now. Thus, at least this stanza brings the RV to 7000 BC. The stanza runs thus:

devá-hitim jugupur dvādaśásya
ṛtum náro ná prá minanty ete,
saṃvatsaré praāvṛṣy āgatāyām
taptā gharmā aśnuvate visargám

"They have guarded the divine order of the year; these creatures do not infringe the time. In a year, the rain having come, the hot sweat gets release".

Here it is interesting to note that náras is at the very early stage of its semantic development, and means just 'creature', not 'men' (Macdonell) or Herren (Geldner) or netāras (Sāyaṇa). As a matter of fact, náras is the reduced inflexional form from the agglutinative ṇara-ṣa, the pl. form of nara- (a creature) which was earlier a phrase (the walking animal), contracted form of the clause ṇa ra (a creature walks) of the isolating stage.

Though the language is very old both morphologically and semantically, it does not point to any period. But the evidence of the astronomy puts it at 7000 BC.

It appears that the agglutinative Indus had just transited to the inflexional stage (ṇara-ṣa : náras), but in meaning the word náras was still limping near the agglutinative stage. It still referred to 'creature, animal' and the new meaning 'a man' was still farther away. Thus the period of the RV centres round 7000 BC, which may also go earlier.

A language which is more perfect than Greek, more copious than Latin and more exquisitely refined than either is said to be younger than Greek!

6

Language-types and Their Proper Scripts

There are fewer writing systems than the number of languages in the world. There are some settled views on the evolution of the ancient scripts. The languages had come to writing at very advanced stages of their evolution.

It is said that there are three stages in the evolution of writing, with two intermediate sub-stages. First of all, when certain languages were required to be written, only words representing certain objects or ideas were pictographed. Thus each picture was a logograph. In this system of writing, the symbols were bound to match with the number of words representing certain object or ideas. We do not find any difficulty in reading the modern universal logographs through any language. For example, 2 + 2 = 4 (two plus two is-equal-to four) reads very well through any language. But in this writing system the numbers of symbols may go to any extent. For its limited use, there were nearly 500 logographs in the ancient Egyptian writing. There are more than 4000 symbols in the modern Chinese. And so on.

At a later stage of the logographic writing, only the first syllable of the word was represented by that logograph. This was the beginning of the sub-stage logosyllabic writing, which culminated in the syllabic script. Many scripts stopped at this stage and remained syllabic for all times to come, even though their shapes changed differently for different languages. But in many other cases, the symbols began to represent single sounds, vowels and consonants, and the script became alphabetic; for example, the Greek and Roman letters from the phoenician writing.

It may be supposed that in the earliest form of the Brāhma script, the object aja (goat) was logographically pictographed as  , representing its remarkable horns. Later it represented only the first syllable a- and was also differently projected as  . Similarly, gaja (elephant) was logographically represented by the whole massive body of the elephant. Later its first syllable ga was written  Thus it can be shown that all Brāhma symbols in their most primitive form were logographs. But the extant Brāhma writing represents a yery advanced civilisation in the human history. It represents the logographs of the underivable bisyllabic words which belong to some ur-Sanskrit. The 'goat' was called aja because its bleating was heard as such in ur-Sanskrit. The elephant was called gaja because its roaring produced a voiced guttural sound. And so on. Many of these ur-Sanskrit words, even though not used, are preserved in the Sanskrit lexicons.

But the traditional Sanskrit lexicons also preserve many monosyllabic words, now hardly used in Sanskrit; e.g. ka 'turtle', ca 'moon', da 'mountain', etc. Just as the bisyllabic underivable words belong to ur-Sanskrit, the monosyllabic words belong to its more primitive form. Fortunately, a good number of these objects have been pictographed in the Indus script and, therefore, we may believe that  'turtle' represents ka, 'moon' represents ca,  'mountains' represents da,  'spider' represents ba,  'bee' represents bha, and so on.

If Sanskrit is inflexional, the ur-Sanskrit was agglutiantive, because it is reasonably supposed that the inflexional language has evolved from the agglutinative stage of the same language. If the ur-Sanskrit, having underivable bisyllabic words was agglutinative, the more primitive language of the Indus inscriptions having monosyllabic words was isolating, the parent of the ur-Sanskrit.

As we look at the texts of the Indus inscriptions, we are surprised to see that there are lines mostly containing three, two or even one symbol, although there are many longer texts too. Here we confront a prehistorical language. We are obliged to think that in the prehistorical language, a clause consisted of a verb alone, and the Sanskrit tradition knows it, defining a clause as "eka-tiṅ vākyam" (a verb is the clause)

When a primitive man saw a river, he just said: na 'it flows' It was only action which first came into his mind. Later, the verb became a noun and, acting as subject, it required another verb da 'makes indistinct noise'. Thus nada was an extended clause, meaning: the flowing object (river) makes indistinct noise. Sometime later, this clause contracted as the phrase 'the noisy river' and then as the lexeme 'river' nada-, f. nadī. Though the usual order of words in the prehistoric clause was the subject (actor) + verb (action), the verb was the pivot round which other words turned up. Thus the verb gā (goes) was also followed by an oblique idea in the form of va (in the dwelling), and gā va too contracted as gāva f. gāvī (known to Patañjali).

Though the primitive man did not realise it, he used to employ two distinct types of verbs in his clause: one was plain, which could not answer the querry 'what'; the other could answer this querry. The other type naturally invited the idea of an 'object' (something acted upon). Therefore, at a later stage, there was an extended clause: subject (actor) + object (the thing acted upon) + verb (action). If anything other than the subject and object came into his mind, it was put at the first position, pushing the subject to the next position.

That is to say, the language of the Indus inscriptions is isolating, the parent of the ur-Sanskrit and the grandmother of the Vedic language.

It is remarkable that even in the primitive form of the Indus language three types of script have been employed in writing the Indus inscriptions. Because the isolating stage of the Indus language had monosyllabic words and each syllable stood for certain physical objects, animals, birds, insects, etc., the first portraying of the Indus syllables was through animal figures. Later the animal figures turned into the geometrical figures. When the qualities of the syllables and their places of utterance were exactly determined, the numerals were invented.

The Indus script was syllabic and comfortable for the language as long as it was agglutinative. That is to say, the isolating language of the Indus inscriptions matched properly with the three varieties of the Indus script. Even the agglutinative stage would have been comfortable for it. But when the language transited into the inflexional stage, the syllabic script became uncomfortable for the language. For centuries, the Vedic literature remained śruti and could not be put to writing.

The grassroot of the society, however, spoke the later form of the agglutinative Indus, the socalled ur-Sanskrit.

Though the tradition of the Indus script was broken due to certain natural calamity, its memory was not dead. Therefore, there was a new attempt to fabricate logographs through the words of the ur-Sanskrit. In this way, the early form of the Brāhma script came into being and began to be employed for the popular language.

The Vedic literature could not remain śruti for a long time. When the Brāhmaṇa literature came into being, it was not possible to memorise them. They were forced to use the Brāhma script, which was being used from the time immemorial at the grassroot of the society. For them, it was created by Brahmā himself. The missing graphemes were reconstructed and the absence of the mark for the bare consonant was put up with.

On the other hand, the syllabary of the Indus language had already been systematised through the invention of the numeral script and was continuing through the oral tradition. When the Brāhma script was adapted for Sanskrit, the old syllabary was copied down in the name of the Māheśvarasūtras.

Thus the Indus script goes to a hoary past. On astronomical grounds, the RV 7,103,9 goes to 7000 BC. Then the grandmother of the Vedic language, the language of the Indus inscriptions, must be three times as old.

Though Sanskrit has reached the inflexional stage typologically, it is continuing with its syllabic script. It is very comfortable to write Sanskrit in the Nāgarī script, but when we come to the analysis of the Sanskrit forms, we feel that some alphabetic script would have been more practical. For example, in budh + s, when the final s is lost and the preceding dh is deaspirated (and devoiced) to t, the aspiration is thrown back on the preceding syllable, so that the result is bhut. With the syllabic script, where the voiced aspirate is written intègrally as one symbol, this transparency of the phonemes is not visible. Because the teaching of the Sanskrit grammar was oral, this process was active in mind, but now when it is taught on a board, a transparent alphabetic script may be more practical.

It is meant to say that though the logographic script is the most primitive form of writing, it is even now useful in certain code-expression. The syllabic script is practical for the languages of the agglutinative type and even for those having syllables closed by vowels. But for the synthetic and analytic languages, with words ending with consonants, the alphabetic writing is the most suitable.

7

The Objective Bases of Decipherment

Though we talk of scientific method in research, it is generally with an 'abrupt find' that the genuine research starts. If there is nothing like an abrupt find, we start with a hypothesis and test its validity on approved grounds. If it proved wrong, we start with a new hypothesis.

We need not go into the criticism of the IE philology, which not only forestalled the path of enquiry into the origin of the Ursprache but even went on to distort the history and related disciplines with its presumptuous inferences.

Sri Aurobindo had reasonably argued that if the linguistics is to be called a science, it has to follow the ways of sciences. It should have gone to the next step only after confirming the first. If *akvas was the original form for áśva, aspa, equus, hippos etc., its existence should have been confirmed. But it did not so happen. While it remained a hoax, apart from various improvements upon it (so that it is now ekwos), even other hoax forms were created on the same model. But a language does not originate in the way the socalled proto-IE has been reconstructed. Patañjali had warned long ago not to create a language just as a potter makes a jar. If we want to know the original form of some cognate words, we should go to the seed-sound from which it has spread, not uniformly but differently in different languages. Just as a grass grows from stem to stem, from one knot to another, a word grows syllable by syllable.

About the origin of the words for 'horse' in the different cognate languages, the following appears to be the process in the manner of the linguistic embryology: originally it was h̲a (a voiceless h), referring to a certain breed of the horse, perhaps so called because its neighing was heard something like h. The traditional Sanskrit lexicons have referred to ha meaning 'horse', perhaps culed from some language, consisting of only monosyllabic words, related with Sanskrit. As its breed was improved in India, it was extended by śa (injury) and va (strength): *h̲a-śa-va (a horse, injurious and strong). In course of time, it was reduced to á-ś-va. The voiceless h was lost at the beginning (probably due to the following ś) and the penultimate a on śa was lost due to accent on the first syllable. Its another breed was extended by ra (speed) and va (strength) and, in the same way, it finally emerged as árvā (a horse, fast and strong), later conceived as árvan in Vedic. But the original *h̲a-r-va underwent a cross-breed with another variety of the horse, namely gand- (which we see in gardabhá 'an ass'), and gandharvá is almost a mythical name for the horse. As the same horse proceeded to Iran, perhaps a new breed emerged, called *h̲a-ś-pha (from *ha-śapha) 'a horse with the injurious hoofs'. In Avesta, it is aspa. The Latin equus, Greek hippos and Germanic *hors were similarly extended, but h was retained in Greek and Germanic. Thus we see that the words for 'horse' did not come in the way it has been reconstructed for IE.

The word for 'cow' originated in a different way. As the language was at the isolating stage, a verb gā was followed by the word va in oblique case, gā va meaning 'goes into the pen'. It contracted as a phrase gāva 'going into the pen'. Then it became a lexical word, its feminine form being gāvī (also known to Patañjali). This gāva- made the pl. gāva-ṣa at the agglutinative stage. At the inflexional stage it was reduced as gāvas due to accent and was analysed as gāv-as, postulating a strong base gāu-. In weak cases, the base was gau- before vowels and go- before consonants.

In the decipherment of the Indus inscription, where both the language and the script are unknown, we are desired to be more objective to escape being misled. It was desirable first of all to know the language, but the first means of knowing the language, however, is the script itself, because it is the frame in which the language has been put.

Just as a square peg in a round hole is uncomfortable, a language fit for the alphabetic script is uncomfortable in the syllabic script. By the time of the development of inflexional Vedic, the script used for its agglutinative and isolating predecessors had become redundant or uncomfortable though the popular dialects were written through it. Therefore, the Vedic literature had to become śruti. But when the Vedic literature became too vast to be preserved in memory, the syllabic Brāhma script was employed with some additions and emendations. Though two consonants could be joined inside the sentence, at the end it had to be written as full syllable. Throughout the Brāhma script this inconvenience was to be put up with. It was only at the Nāgarī stage that a trick called halanta was invented to mark the bare consonant.

Though the stages in the development of script are described as logographic, syllabic and alphabetic, the real order of the stages is syllabic and alphabetic, the former suitable for the isolating and agglutinative and the latter for the inflexional and the modern analytic languages. The logographic script developed all at once at the advanced stage of some language when it was desired to be recorded.

As we look at the Indus texts, we find that each sign is a syllable, which is evident by its standing alone:

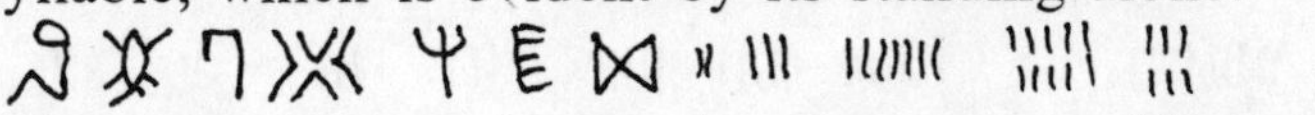

The same sign stands even in groups, also without taking any diacritical mark. It shows that it is a syllable. The syllables are grouped in pairs and triplets, and they are perhaps clauses. If there are more than two or three syllables in a line, we suppoşe, it is another regrouping: the first two or three making one clause, and the next making another clause.

Perhaps we have recognised the type of the language represented by the Indus texts just on the basis of the graphic form. It is a language at the isolating stage. Each syllable is a word and, though even one syllable states some action with the status of a verb, two or three syllables certainly make a clause.

As regards the means to know the phonemic value of the syllables, there is some dependable clue: If the syllabic order of Māheśvarasūtras at the beginning of the Pāṇini's grammar is put on the numerals of specific shapes and lengths, it covers all the signs.

It is in the following way, specially with respect to the consonants, because the Sanskrit school had interfered with the order of the Indus vowels, which had considerably changed by the time of Pāṇini:

10 9 8 7 6 5 4 3 2 1

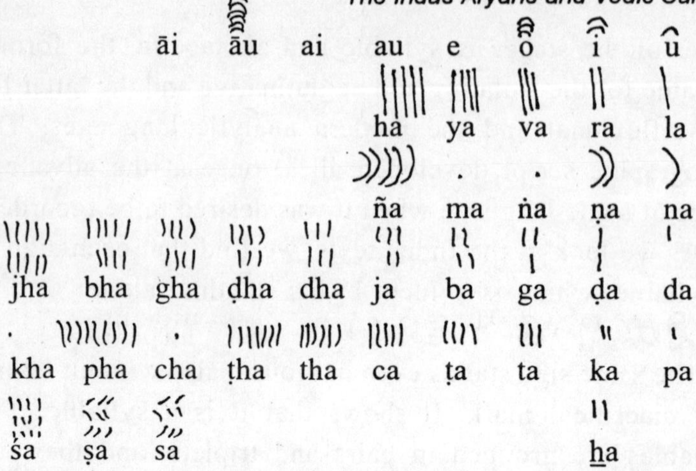

Even the traditional Sanskrit lexicons of the monosyllabic words offer some help: some syllables refer to some animals, birds, insects and physical objects, and they have been pictographed in the Indus scripts; e.g. mountain da, bee bha, dog ḍha, spider ba, bird sa, leaf pa, turtle ka, moon ca, drum ḍa, breast ta, arrow va, and nipple ṣa.

With this marginal help, we read as ta na ṣa. A slightly deviating` , and also present the same syllabic group. This ta na ṣa reflects in the Vedic tánas (offspring), which helps in understanding ta (womb) na (gem) ṣa (embryo) as a clause meaning 'from the womb gems come out'.

This leader of the Indus texts leads us to many other:

 ṇa ga (light movement) = The light is going away (i.e. the darkness is coming). It has fossilised as nág (night) in the RV (7,71,1).

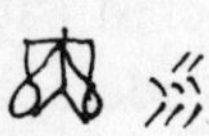 ṣa ṭha (embryo circle) = The ball rolled. It has been paraphrased in the RV: hiraṇya-garbhaḥ sam-avartatāgre (the golden ball rolled forth). The clause itself has phonetically fossilised as

sát, but it was later confused with the participal sát from as 'to be'.

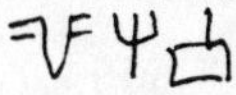 va ṇa ṣa (water life embryo) = From the water the life comes. It was reduced to vánas in vanas-pati (plant).

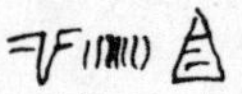 h̠a ṭha ṣa (empty-space disc embryo) = From the empty space a ball emerged. It has fossilised as satás in sató-vīra -bṛhat and -mahat.

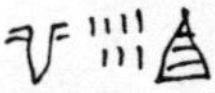 h̠a ḍha sa (empty-space sound embryo) = In the empty space there was big bang. It is sadha (heaven) in the RV.

 la ṭha (time disc) = The time turns round. It has fossilised as ṛtá (the regular order of the universe) in the RV.

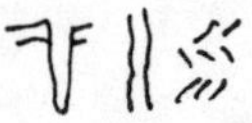 ṣa ra ṣa (nipple speed end) = Flows from the mountain and stops on the way. Its reduced form is sáras (pond, lake, sea), the first element in the name Sarasvatī

These clauses consist of subject + verb, oblique-case + subject + verb, and subject + object + verb, though other possibilities are there, namely verb + oblique-case (gā va 'goes into the pen'), oblique-case + verb (bī ja 'from the water it grows'), etc.

Clearly, three types of scripts have been used in the Indus inscriptions: animal figures, geometrical figures and numerals. By the mutual help of these three scripts in duplicate and triplicate texts, almost all basic signs of the Indus script have been recognised as specific syllables:

Māheśvarasūtras	*Animal figure*	*Geometrical figure*	*Numeral*
ha			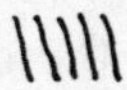
ya			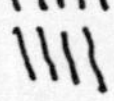

va
ra
la
ña
ṇa
na
jha
bha
gha
ḍha
dha
ja
ba
ḍa
da
kha
pha
cha
ṭha
tha
ca
ṭa
ta
ka
pa
śa
ṣa
sa
ẖa

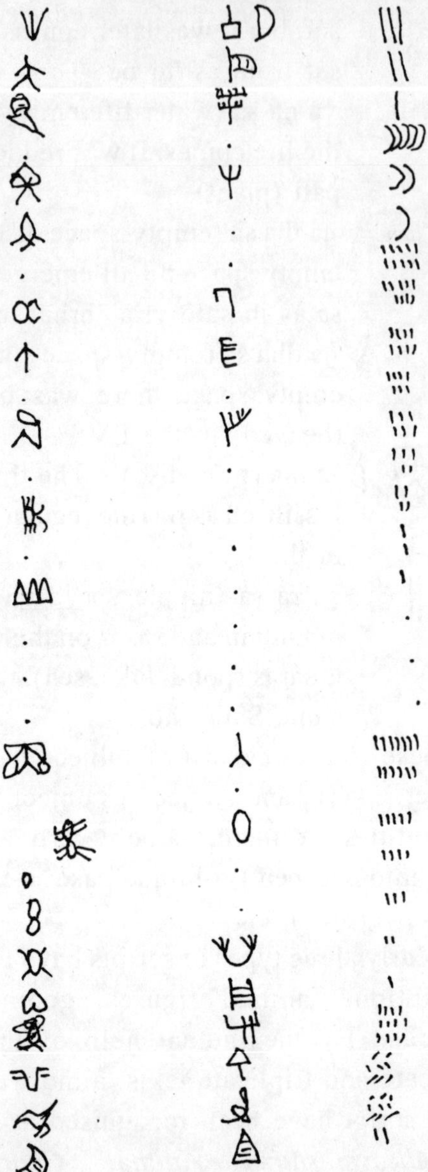

Because the animal figures are generally not prepared to take the diacritical marks, vowels other than the consonant represented by it has been slightly modified. Thus, though the ant- sign has seven occurrences in all, it has six variants. Therefore, the compilers of the Indus script may be advised to copy even a slight variation as a sign representing specific syllables.

The vowels have been recognised through their association with specific consonants. A text was provisionally read rau ra which appeared to reflect in a rare Vedic vocable rūrá 'heat of fever'. Because adding a sign from two sides was conceived as a primitive way of making a long vowel, was read as ra-ū. In this way, was conceived to be i in ra-i, and its long form was seen in ga-ī, also seen without a consonant in the middle ,which identified another ī in a duplicate text. Even though without any solid confirmation, has been read as o and as h̲a-ō. Then perhaps is e and is ra-ē. Because is a long ī, its simple form may be i, and in ri is its diacritical form. On the basis of in , probably yu, a sign V has been assumed for u, even though not attested. On this basis has been read as va, just as appears to be va through for u.

Thus we may be supposed to have partly read the Indus inscriptions and also to have understood a major portion of them. We do not only have a complete idea of the structure of the language, which was then at the isolating stage, but we can also explore its way to the inflexional stage through the agglutinative stage. Thus the poet Jaya Shankar Prasad had truly said:

> We had not come from anywhere else:
> Our homeland was here itself.

The Indian history should be rewritten and the language of India should be resurveyed.

8

On the Gradual Decipherment of the Indus Script

A reviewer of books on the decipherment of the Indus script starts with calling it "arbitrary", even if it appears to be reasonable to some extent. Because even the language is not known, it becomes difficult to justify the procedure. Though any visibility is the result of a sudden flash of light, if it relates to some mental revelation it is hardly called a "scholarship". But it is often this sudden flash of light which shows the path continuously.

The monosyllabic words of the traditional Sanskrit lexicons (Ekākṣara-koṣa) compiled in the modern Sanskrit dictionaries have given several meanings of each syllable of the Sanskrit alphabet. Out of them, the following syllables with a̲ have certain meaning which can be pictographed. For example, da= mountain, bha = bee, ca = moon, ḍha = dog, ba = spider (tantu-santāna), sa = bird, pa = leaf, ka = turtle, ḍa = drum, ṇa = pānīya-nilaya (residing in waters), ta = breast, va = arrow, and ṣa = nipple

As the first step in my decipherment, these pictographs were identified with the respective sounds as follows : mountain da, bee bha, dog ḍha, spider ba, bird sa, leaf pa, turtle ka, moon ca, drum ḍa, breast ta, arrow va, and nipple ṣa. The various "fish" signs could be identified with different sounds later on. The pānīya-nilaya (fish) for ṇa proved to be misleading.

There are some other animal figures in the Indus script, but the traditional lexicons do not offer any help: the hind-leg of a horse, a watchman, the neck of the human being, the back and shoulder of a sitting man, a bat, a bearer, an ant, a hare or squirrel, two eyes of an animal, a water bird, and two more not identifiable.

There are a few more animal figures, but they have been drawn geometrically: two horns along with the head of an animal, another two horns in the form of U or V, and some others of controversial shapes , etc.

For quite some time, the first "fish" sign was conceived as ṇa (pānīya-nilaya 'residing in waters'), but it proved to be wrong, because it turned out to be the dental na by comparison with the corresponding numeral in the duplicate texts. The mistake would have crept in due to wrong oral transmission of the sound.

Though the meaning 'nipple' has been assigned to ṣa and could be identified as such, this value could be assigned to it in an indirect way.

Once, in the middle of the year 1996, I happened to see the same 5-sign text partly written in two ways:

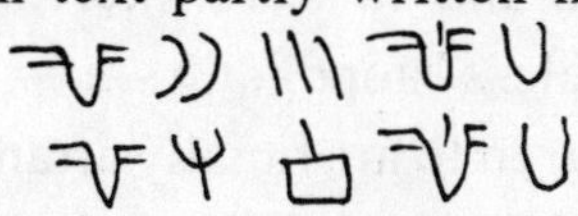

After a rigorous exercise, it came out that the 3rd and 4th from the right in each line are va and ṇa respectively, This discovery led to the identification of the specific ascending order of the numerals from right to left with the syllabic order of the Māheśvarasūtras, read in the reverse order, from left to right.

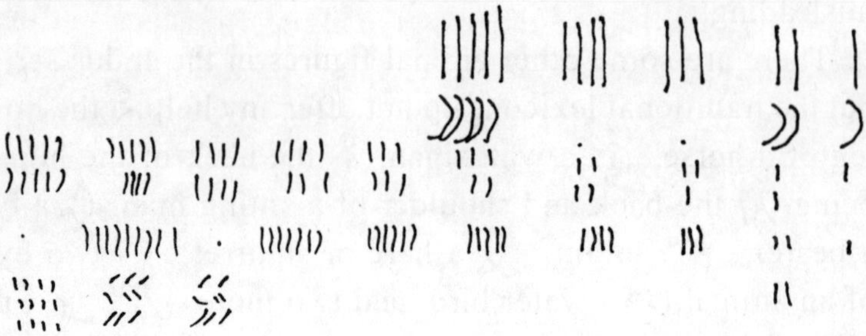

This order matched wonderfully with the syllabic order of the Māheśvarasūtras, with minor aberrations carried out by the Sanskrit school.

The syllabic order of the Māheśvarasūtras for the consonants is the following.

					ha	ya	va	ra	la
					ña	ma	ṅa	ṇa	na
jha	bha	gha	ḍha	dha	ja	ba	ga	ḍa	da
kha	pha	cha	ṭha	tha	ca	ṭa	ta	ka	pa
śa	ṣa	sa						ha	

The Sanskrit school had probably interchanged the places of kha and cha to keep kha pha and ka pa at the two ends of the voiceless stops having the corresponding sibilants. Even the places of ṣa and sa were interchanged to match the order of the voiceless stops.

The numerals appeared to artificially arrange the syllables of the Indus language based on their qualities and places of utterance. The ur-Māheśvarasūtras were probably arranged on the basis of the relative frequency of sounds in the original language. That is why, the last used sounds like jha cha were put at the 10th place. Otherwise, it would have been difficult to write the texts in the numeral script.

The vowels are poorly represented through the numerals, and the Sanskrit school adopted them after some editing, for which Pāṇini even apologised by highlighting u, the first vowel of the Indus phonology. The original order of the Indus phonology, namely u i o e au ai āu āi, was broken into 4 groups, namely 1 u i 2 o e 3. au ai 4. āu āi, and each time the order was reversed: i u e o ai au āi āu. Then putting a at the head, and replacing e o (which had gone out of use) by ṛ l (which had newly developed from ra la), the vowels were written thus: 1 a i u 2. ṛ l 3. e o (from the original ai au) 4. ai au (from the original āi āu).

The numeral signs for the vowels are the following:  u i  o  āu

With the identification of the numerals with the syllabic order of the Māheśvarasūtras, almost one-third of signs was identified.

This discovery proved that Sanskrit is in the genealogical line of the Indus language. Just on the basis of the graphic form of the inscriptions it could be imagined that if Sanskrit is the final stage of the development of the language, the language of the inscriptions is the initial stage.

In the duplicate writing like those above, some other signs were identified. It gradually appeared that the inscriptions have been written in three scripts: the writing started with the animal figures, the most natural way of turning sounds into symbols. After gradual refinement in the animals figures, the geometrical figures were invented. When the phonetic system was well established, they arranged the sounds according to qualities through the various shapes and sizes of the numerals and observing the ascending order from right to left in respect of the places of utterance, also taking care of the fact that the least used sound were placed at the end. Thus we see that the number "2" stands for at least 6 sounds :  i ra  ṇa ḍa  ka  h̲a

The phoneticians of the Indus school had put the stops in the strict order of the places of utterance, but the Sanskrit school undertook some editing with regard to the phonetic situation in Sanskrit. They interchanged the places of kha and cha, which are fortunately for us not even represented in the script, so that "cha ṭha tha ca ṭa ta" were flanked by "kha pha" and "ka pa" from two sides, the latter having no corresponding sibilants and the former having śa ṣa sa in order. Accordingly, there was also some change in the order of the sibilants, ṣa put in the middle, while originally it headed the group of three sibilants and also stood for 3, which is the basis of the number 6 = ṣa 3 + ṣa 3 (becoming ṣáṣ in Sanskrit due to accent)

Because there were two h-phonemes in the Indus syllabary, the one at the beginning of the consonants and the other at the end, ha stood for 2. This ha is the basis of the older dual forms: gāva-ha gāva-H gāvā. The laryngeal H of the Indoeuropeanists lies in the ruins of the Indus phonology.

As regards the frequency of the symbols, the simple ones used to outnumber the complex ones, without any regard to the animal, geometrical and numeral figures.

With the help of the numerals, the first "fish"  was identified as na:  .

 The second "fish" was identified as ma: 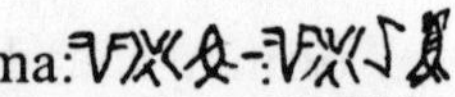

 The third "fish" was identified as ha: 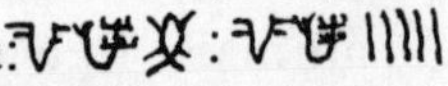

The fourth fish was identified as jha without any proof, though jhaṣa means 'fish'. 

Among the next group of the animal figures, was identified as ra on the basis of the clause raura reflecting in a rare Vedic vocable rūrá (heat of the fever). The sign was identified as la through a rustic word lathār (the strike by the hind-leg of an animal). The sign was identified as ṇa through a rare text ṇaga (the light went away), which reflects in a rare Vedic vocable nág (night). The sign was identified as gha on the basis of the rustic words gheṭ, ghegh, etc. (pointing to the region of the neck). The sign was read dha through a rustic word for the region of the body, attested by some Vedic words. The sign was read as ja in jatu (a bat), being probably the Indus word for that creature. The sign portrays a 'bearer' or 'porter', and its identification with ṭha was based on the ligature ṣ-ṭa and ṣ-ṭha. The sign stands for ca through the creature cītī (ant) It occurs 7 times in all, but has six variants for the different vowels attached to it. The sign stands for śa through śaśa for *śa-sa (long-eared), though śa could also indicate squirrel.

The geometrical signs too were similarly identified in the duplicate texts, either through the numerals or the animal figure. Thus pa was seen in the following: . pa ka ṣa. bha was seen in the following: . na bha ṣa; and the long ī was seen in the following: . īka ṣa. This text also gave clue to the formation of the long vowels. Just as the plural was formed by the repetition of the signs, the long vowel was indicated by putting the same sign from two sides.

The identification of so many signs gave impetus to read certain texts with great certainty.

The text ta na ṣa, written in four ways, . . .

appeared to have fossilised as tánas (offspring), occurring only once in the RV (4,70,5). This correspondence of ta na ṣa and tánas appeared to suggest that the Vedic language is the final stage of the language which is represented in the Indus inscriptions: if tánas represented the inflexional stage, ta na ṣa must represent the isolating stage.

There are three stages in the development of a language, namely isolating, agglutinative and inflexional. The isolating stage of a language has no grammar, as is clearly to be seen in ta na ṣa. The specific order of the monosyllabic words explain their status as subject, object or verb. Because the Indus texts are very small, they are evidently little clauses made of subject + verb, subject + object + verb, oblique case + subject + verb, and their various manipulations to express various ideas. On the basis of the lexicons of the monosyllabic words and from the meaning derived from the fossilised Vedic word tánas, the Indus text ta na ṣa seems to give the following meaning; from the womb (of a woman) gems come out. It could also mean: the womb of a woman brings out gems.

The gap between the isolating language of the Indus texts and the inflexional Vedic should have been filled up by some language of the agglutinative type, where the grammatical elements would have appeared. In the extant inscriptions themselves, there are certain sign-pairs, the second part of which appear to be the affix element. It seems that by the time of the isolating language of the Indus society coming into writing, it had moved towards the agglutinative stage. Two grammatical elements, gha for future and ga for order are seen in large number. A text dra-gha,  ra ga (conflagration-future, speed-order) seems to say: There will be a catastrophic fire; do run away. In the inscriptions, as a part of the longer texts, there are rare instances of ṭha for the past tense (which was dentalised and deaspirated as -ta in Vedic). Though not fully confirmed, there is ra for pluperfect (a pluperfect form ca-ra 'had taken place' noted by Pāṇini as a secondary suffix in the sense of bhūta-pūrva 'former') and ha for perfect (a perfect form ma-ha 'has grown old' making a clause tata maha 'the father has grown old' which contracted as a word tatāmaha grandfather', its last part -maha appearing as suffix in pitā-maha 'grandmother', etc.)

It is surprising that those affix elements of Indus, ha for perfect (he has gone) and ra for pluperfect (he had gone) are still surviving in the rustic dialects of India. The affix gha for future is still continuing in Hindi in its deaspirated form gā.

The language of the Aśokan inscriptions is just a form of the agglutinative Indus, which was coming limping at the grassroot of the Indian society in the 3rd century BC. It is not the socalled old Prakrit, and its study should be carried out in its special relation with the Munda and Dravidian languages as well.

As the Indus language was crossing the border of the isolating stage, there was some natural catastrophe in the whole region. The community disintegrated in several groups. The southern group went to the extreme south, in the country of the hot sun, dra-vi-ḍa or dra-mi-ḍa as they called it (and the word Tamil is derived from it). The eastern group went to the hills and forests of the central India. The northern group went to the land watered by the seven rivers, and the western group went to the land of the Soma plant on Iran-Afghan border.

Under the unfavourable natural conditions in the south and east, the Indus language remained limping at the agglutinative stage. That is to say, it never reached the inflexional stage. But in the land of the Soma plants and seven rivers, under the favourable conditions of nature, the language crossed the agglutinative stage and became accented. It was the inflexional Indus.

A group of population of the land of soma plants proceeded towards central Asia on their way to Europe, carrying with them the voiced and voiceless h (preserved in Hittite, which were normalised in Vedic, though reflecting in the duals). A break-away group of the land of the Soma plants later merged with the people of the land of seven rivers and laid the foundation of the Vedic culture.

A number of texts in the extent Indus inscriptions can be shown to have evolved as fossilised vocables of the Vedic language 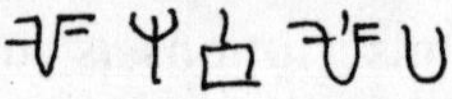 ga ṣu va ṇa ṣa = Plants grow because the water gives life.

What is a clause in the Indus inscriptions has become a wornout and reduced vocable in the Vedic language.

śa ma yo ṣa has fossilised as śáṃ yós

ca na ṣa has fossilised as cánas.

ra bī ṣu va ṇa ṭha has fossilised as ṛbīsa vanád (two rare words in the Vedic vocabulary).

A very small text 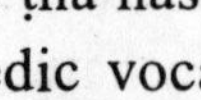 ṣa ṭha (embryo circle 'the ball rolled forth') has been reparaphrased in the RV: hiraṇya-garbhaḥ sam-avartatāgre.

It is not a place to show all the examples.

The most revealing fact is that the Indus syllabary as seen in the Māheśvarasūtras is the basis of the IE numerals from 5 to 10: proceeding from the end of the Māheśvarasūtras (from the beginning of the Indus syllabary) and running forward, we find that h̲a covers 7 syllables upto ta via p, and therefore h̲a-p-ta = 7 (hapta in Avesta, but sapta in Sanskrit); h̲a covers 8 syllables upto ṭa via ṣ, and therefore h̲a-ṣ-ṭa = 8 (aṣṭa in Sanskrit, but *hašta in Iranian, hasht in modern Persian); ṣa stands for 3, therefore ṣaṣa (3+3) = 6 (ṣáṣ in Sanskrit) ; pa covers 5 syllables upto ca, and putting the 5th nasal ñ in the middle, pa-ñ-ca = 5 (because c was also pronounced as affricate /tś./, Gk has pente); from na to va (including the unwritten anusvāra), there are 9 syllables, therefore na-va = 9; and from da to jha there are 10 syllables, therefore, the affricate jh = dzh losing its aspiration and stop element and z devoiced to ś, da-śa = 10. In the western Indus dialects, jh was velarised, devoiced and deaspirated; thus Latin decem, Gk deka, etc.

Thus the language underneath the Indus script is the grandmother of the Vedic language and, as a whole, the ancestor of the IE languages. It is the most primitive form of the human speech.

The animal script shows the natural wealth of the Indus people; the geometrical script show their technical skill; and the numerals betray their scientific mind.

The script beginning with animals in their original form in the early Indus writing indicates, among other things, the economic value of the specific animals in the most primitive form of their society. Though by the time of the writing of the inscriptions, they had advanced in culture, they did not forget the primitive form of their beginning. Therefore, some of the animal figures show the tribal form of the society.

The nipple sign indicated the profuseness of the milch cattle. The several varieties of birds and fish indicate the wealth relating to forest and water. Some people were archers, and the dogs were their means of hunting. They cultured bees for honey. The spider could indicate the production of cloths in large quantities. The skull of a turtle was fashioned into a club for fighting. The leaf of the pipal tree was their initial dish for food. The drum was the first musical instrument. A horse has been portrayed through its hind-leg whose strike is welknown even today. The long-eared hare or squirrel should have been favourite animals. A man  , representing ra (speed, fire), was the most active and ruthless being of the society, who could also be employed as a strong watchman or a porter (continuing till 50 years ago in the countryside). Some sign refers to asceticism.

This script was quite suitable for the isolating and agglutinative stage of the language, but when the inflexional Vedic emerged, it became quite unsuitable. Therefore the Vedic literature had to become śruti. But when the Vedic literature became very bulky, the Brāhma script, devised for the popular language after a tremenous gap of time, was employed, adding the missing graphemes, even if it was not quite suitable for it. Here, however, the horn of a goat 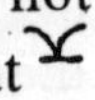 for a̲ (from aja) has been wonderfully drawn  . It was no more an animal figure.

9

On the Chronology of the Indus Script

It looks very odd to write the chronology of the evolution of the Indus script without claiming to have it deciphered. Even if one claims to have deciphered it, partly or fully, it is difficult to go to its history, because it is not possible to say which is earlier and which is later. But one may get a glimpse of the history in the manner of the its being deciphered or identified. Though history is an art, its base is scientific, because one event follows another in a natural way. Therefore, it may not be difficult to state the relative chronology of the signs of the Indus script as they gradually came into being. There are, according to Mahadevan

	419	basic signs
(-)	179	signs having variants
	240	
(+)	641	variants of the 179 signs
	881	total number of the signs (a few more or

less on account of the missing or duplicate signs).

Though Mahadevan has classified them variously, three main types are easily discernible. They are:

1. animal figures
2. geometrical figures

3. numerals

These three types indicate the natural chronology of their development. An enlightened human society cannot ignore the animals, birds and physical objects of the surrounding from its observation. Therefore the first syllables to be pictographed would have been through the animal figures.

According to Mahadevan's observation, 1-84 signs represent the animal figures. He has ignored some others, which might be the animal figures in their advanced state of depiction, almost bordering on the geometrical figures.

The insight to recognise these animal figures to represent some syllables came from the traditional Sanskrit lexicons, compiled in the modern Sanskrit dictionaries, which ascribe some meanings to individual syllables. Some of the syllables are said to refer to some animals, birds, insects, physical objects, namely: ka turtle, ca moon, ḍha dog, da mountain, pa leaf, ba spider, bha bee. There is no doubt that, at the beginning of the human speech, when only syllables could have been uttered by those human beings, every syllable would have referred to animals, birds, insects and physical objects. Unfortunately, they all have not come down to us in entirety. At least these few are pictographed in the Indus script:  turtle,  moon,  dog, 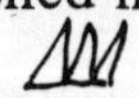 mountain,  leaf,  spider,  bee.

One is very likely to conceive that the syllables said to mean specific beings might belong to some prehistoric language, and that prehistoric language, if it was Indus itself, might have employed them for its use in the enlightened society.

This is the foundation on which the chronology of the origin of the Indus script can be reconstructed. It makes us conceive that the Indus script can be reconstructed. It makes us conceive that the Indus language had monosyllabic word and, if the syllable of the Māheśvarasūtras may be said to have briefly preserved that prehistoric phonology in a little modified form, there might be 34 consonants x 14 vowels[1] = 476 syllables. They should have stood for various animals, birds, insect and physical objects, and the easier of them have been pictographed to represent those syllables. Thus, at the beginning of the writing, they should have pictographed at least 476 animals, etc. representing specific syllables. But the consonants being conspicuously remarkable, the 476 symbols for signs for those syllables should have been reduced to just 34 for the consonants and 14 for the vowels, some of them replaced or supplemented by diacritical marks.[2] Though all the 34 consonants and 14 vowels have not been preserved or come down to us, we may suppose that they once existed in entirety.

The hints for other syllables represented by the specific animals, etc. are not there in the traditional Sanskrit lexicons. But, surprisingly, some signs or symbols have been identified by the rustic words of the modern vernaculars,[3] e.g. the hind-leg of a horse, the back portion of the body, the throat portion of the neck of a human being, and so on. Sometimes the meaning of the syllables have not been faithfully handed down, which are to be corrected by our personal judgement.[4] Many kinds of fish itself are seen representing specific syllables. That is to say,  = na  = ma 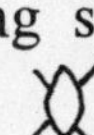 = ha, and probably,  =jha

The animal figures being naturally considered rustic in the eyes of the people of the advancing culture, many of them already transiting to the geometrical shapes, they would have invented the parallel geometrical figure for the corresponding animal figures. Thus, the number of syllables remaining the same, the signs would have been nearly doubled. Unfortunately, the traditional Sanskrit lexicons have not given any hint about the meanings of the geometrical figures. However, with the help of the animal figures in duplicate texts some of the geometrical figures can be recognised. But one cannot claim to have identified all the geometrical figures.

But this is not the end of the Indus cryptography. The society was gradually more enlightened, and the linguistically conscious among the citizens were able to know the qualities and the places of utterance of the syllables. They arranged the syllables according to qualities and places of utterance in a fool-proof way. For this they invented an artificial numeral script in very scientific way. The various shapes of the numerals indicated the specific qualitative types of syllables as noted below:

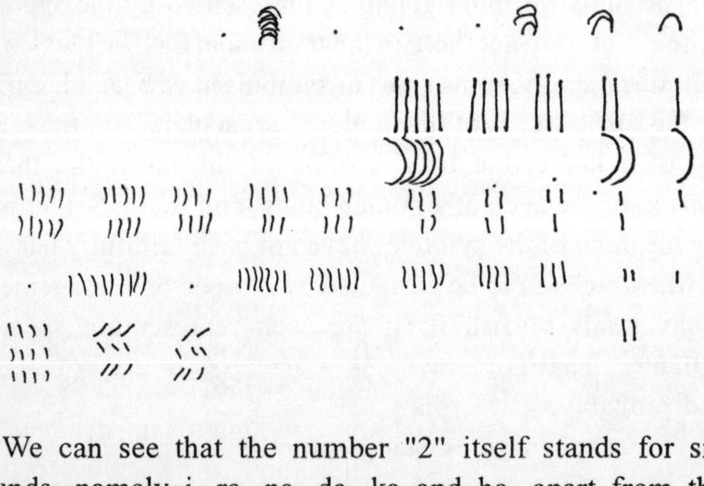

We can see that the number "2" itself stands for six sounds, namely i, ra, ṇa, ḍa, ka and h̲a, apart from the diacritical mark for i.

It is true that we are not able to identify each animal figure with specific syllables, some of them perhaps not represented at all and some others unidentifiable, but historically they may be placed in the first list. Even all the geometrical figures are not represented or, if represented, not identifiable, but we are sure that there would have been geometrical figures for all the syllables. It is only the numerals which fully represent the syllables, the missing ones exactly imaginable.

We are, however, able to discover that the animal figures representing specific syllables were invented first of all, probably to cover the entire syllabary. They were followed by the geometrical figures.

Though some of the geometrical figures are evidently the result of improvement upon the animal figures, some of them are newly drawn. For example, when the animal figure  was finally redrafted as  its geometrical version was unexpectedly . It is only in the rare Indus clauses reflecting in the rare Vedic vocables that such geometrical figures could be identified. Thus  could be identified as ra through 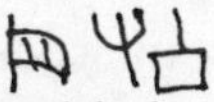 because the first two were already known and the third could make this clause reflect in the Vedic vanar- in vanar-gu and -ṣád, which had been so far wrongly identified with the usual vanas, in spite of the phonetic difficulty. It is sometimes through common sense and sometimes through intuition that some animal and geometrical figures have been approximately identified. It has been very lately realised that because the animal figures were not ready to admit the diacritical marks to show different vowels, the Indus cryptographers changed their shapes for this purpose. Therefore, we see that though the ant-sign has seven occurrences in all, it has six variants. Though initially it was thought to be due to the different hands of the scribes, it is now realised that the change is intentional. Once this fact was realised, it also appeared that· no variant is superfluous. All the extant signs should be represented in the list of the script. The varying number of strokes in the geometrical figures indicate the different vowels attached with a consonant.

However, it has not been so far possible to identify each animal and geometrical figure with the variants, because they can be confirmed to represent certain syllables only when they reflect in some Vedic vocables, which is not always possible.

Notes and references

1. This number of vowels comprises the natural triangle of a i u, short and long, e and o, short and long, in place of the Vedic ṛ l which had developed from ra la, and the original diphthongs ai āi au āu.
2. It appears that the vowels i and u, short and long, added in full make diphthongs (ai aī au aū : āi āu have not been seen), and those added in reduced form or diacritically show the specific vowels, e.g.  ri  yu, etc.
3. Such words are lathār (strike by the hind-leg), dhaonā (back), ghēgh (thyroid gland), etc. for: 
4. For example, pānīya-nilaya (residing in water = fish) should have been for na, which is wrongly said to be for ṇa.

10

A Phonetic Analysis of the Indus Syllabary

The Indus syllabary is supposed to have been preserved very scientifically in the syllabic order of the Māheśvarasūtras, in a little modified form, at the beginning of the Pāṇini's grammar Aṣṭādhyāyī.. Thus the original Indus syllabary is what we may call ur-Māheśvarasūtras. Though the Indus syllabary can be reconstructed even by the animal and geometrical figures, it is numerals which can be properly reasonably identified with the syllabic order of the Māheśvarasūtras.

There was a good deal of editing in case of the vowels of the ur-Māheśvarasūtras. The vowel at the head of the ur-Māheśvarasūtras was u, going from right to left in the following order: u i o e au ai āu āi. It was divided into four groups : 1, u i 2. o e 3. au ai 4. āu āi. The vowel a was not mentioned, because it is inherent in every consonant. Then the order was reversed in each case : i u, e o, ai au, āi āu. Finally, a was put at the head of the first group, for which Pāṇini had to apologise (1, 2, 27) in a decent way. Again, because e o had gone out of use by the time of the RV and ṛ l had appeared as new vowels from ra la, the former were replaced by the latter. Long before Pāṇini, ai au had contracted as the monophthongs e o and āi āu were reduced to ai au, though their original value was known to the grammarians. Therefore the order of the vowels in the Māheśvarasūtras is the following: 1. a i u 2. ṛ l 3. e o 4. ai au.

It is difficult to say whether the consonant series began with the voiced h or with the voiceless h̲. From the Pāṇinian adaptation it appears that the series began with the voiced h, in the following groups, as follows.

					ha	ya	va	ra	la
					ña	ma	a	ṇa	na
jha	bha	gha	ḍha	dha	ja	ba	ga	ḍa	da
kha	pha	cha	ṭha	tha	ca	ṭa	ta	ka	pa
śa	ṣa	sa						h̲a	

In case of consonants also some amount of editing was carried out by the Sanskrit school. Because the strokes increase in number from right to left, it may be supposed that the most frequent phoneme was placed at the first position in each line. Then it also means that the phonemes at the last position in each line were the least used. Indirectly, it also shows that the semivowels, nasals and unaspirates were the mostly used phonemes, while the aspirates in general had a poor presence in the language.

In the voiceless stop series, the 8th and 10th are not quotable at all, and the 9th is quotable only once. If the places of utterance were taken into account, the 10th should go to cha and the 8th to kha, because in the voiced stop series the 10th goes to jha and 8th to gha. But in the voiceless stop series itself, pa and ka have been represented by smaller strokes, and the order of the voiced stops has not been observed. It appears that pa and ka were correspondingly as numerous as ta and ṭa, which are the 1st and 2nd in their new shape. Because Pāṇini followed the Indus syllabary faithfully, he also thought it reasonable to keep ka pa under a separate sūtra. The voiceless stops differ among themselves in one respect: the labials and gutturals have no corresponding sibilants, while the others do have.

On the authority of Pāṇini, it appears that there was cha on the 8th and kha on the 10th. Perhaps taking the order of the voiceless stops - ch ṭh th : c ṭ t - which have the corresponding sibilants, into account, the order of the sibilants was slightly changed from the Indus ṣa sa śa to the Sanskrit śa ṣa sa.

The IE numerals from 5 to 10 are based on the Indus syllabary going from right to left, from the voiceless h towards the voiced.[3]

Though Pāṇini had quoted the two h-phonemes of the Indus syllabary, the voiceless h and the voiced h, at the two ends of the consonants, the Sanskrit tradition had objected to the pronunciation of h as voiceless (RV-Prātiśākhya 14,28). Pāṇini also remained reticent about the two forms of h. Only the commentators have given some explanation. The two h-sounds, however, reflect through their phonetic changes even in Sanskrit. The phonetic change involved in vah + ta is different from that in vah + sa. Then it appears that the same h was voiced in one situation and voiceless in other. The Vedic hima (winter) appearing as zima in Avesta and the Avestan hapta appearing as sapta in Vedic point to two types of h is the original language. The voiceless and voiced h were established phonemes in the Indus language.

That distinction is still maintained in the Santhal language. Bodding remarkably observes: h, the voiceless, or sometimes voiced, fricative glottal..... in some other Munda language h is used initially in certain words where it does not occur in Santhal; other munda languages such as Kurku have k in many words where Santhali has h.

Something has to be said specifically on the phonetic status of the palatals /c ch j jh/. They were both stops and affricates, either dialectally or situation-wise.

The affricate value of c is evidently clear is pañca 'five' when it is pente in Greek. The Indus verb jān/dzān/ was reduced to dān in the old Persian (modern Persian mī-dān-am 'I know), zān in Avestan, but jān-ā-mi in Sanskrit (wrongly analysed jā-nā-mi). In vedic, jān had contracted to jñā, which is seen in some verbal forms and derivatives. The aspiration and the stop elements of ch/tśh/goes away before na in Sanskrit : pra-ś-na. On the other hand, in Sandhi t and ś combine to become a new affricate cluster: tat + śivam = tac-chivam. The voiced aspirate jh/dzh/ appears differently in different languages. In dadzha for da-jha (ten syllables from da to jha), the stop element and the aspiration have gone and the voiced z has been devoiced in the Sanskrit numeral da-śa 'ten'. In Greek deka and Latin decem, jh was a stop which had been gutturalised, devoiced and deaspirated. In Germanic its aspiration was retained: German zehn, There is aham (I) in Sanskrit, azem in Avesta and adam in old Persian, all of which should go to the Indus a-jha/a-dzha. In the western diaclects, jh was a stop: It was gutturalised and then deaspirated in Greek and Latin ego. It was also devoiced in Germanic: old English ic.

All the nasals were full syllables in Indus, all having specific meanings. In Sanskrit, only na and ma appear as full syllables.

It was not necessary to reconstruct a proto-IE.

Notes and References

1. Three types of script have been employed in the Indus inscriptions: the animal figures, the geometrical figures, and the numerals. It is the numerals which can be identified with a phoneme of the Māheśvarasūtras even where it is missing. There are only four numerals, those for ṅ and m as well as ch and kh, which are missing, but they can be easily imagined through their natural order.
2. The vowels ṛ l are typically Vedic products. That is why, the Vedic ṛtu corresponds to the Avestan ratu, and the Vedic ṛtá may be traced to the Indus clause la ṭha (time circle = the time turns round). These vowels are unnecessary for the proto-IE.
3. The IE numerals from 5 to 10 simply count the syllables of the ur-Māheśvarasūtras:
   from pa to ca there are 5 syllables; therefore, putting the fifth nasal ñ in the middle, pa-ñ-ca = 5.
   ṣa (3) ṣa (3) = ṣaṣa, Vedic ṣáṣ = 6.
   from h̠a to ta there are 7 syllables; therefore, putting -p- in the middle, h̠a-p-ta = 7 (Vedic sapta, Av. hapta)
   from h̠a to ṭa there are 8 syllables; therefore, putting ṣ in the middle, h̠a-ṣ-ṭa = 8 (Vedic aṣṭa, modern Persian hašt).
   from na to va, the nsals, including anusvāra, being a group of six, there are 9 syllables; therefore na-va = 9.
   from da to jha there are 10 syllables; therefore da-jha = 10. But jh being the affricate /dzh/, the stop element and the aspiration being lost and z devoiced, we have da-śa = 10 in Vedic. Elsewhere it was gutturalised, devoiced and deaspirated cf. Greek deka, Latin decem.

11

The Phonetic Arithmetic of the Indus Numeral Signs

It is supposed that the syllabic order of the Māheśvarasūtras at the beginning of the Pāṇinian Aṣṭādhyāyī is an updated and edited version of the Indus syllabary. What follows is the pre-edited Indus syllabary, that is, the ur-Māheśvarasūtras:

1.							ś	s	ṣ	h̲	
2.	kh	ph	ch	ṭh	th		c	ṭ	t	k	p
3.	jh	bh	gh	ḍh	dh		j	b	g	ḍ	d
4.							ñ	m	ṅ	ṇ	n
5.							h	y	v	r	l
6.				āi	āu	ai	au	e	o	i	u

These six series of syllables represent qualitative groups of sounds, namely: 1. the voiceless fricatives, 2. the voiceless stops, 3. the voiced stops, 4. the nasals, 5. the voiced fricatives, and 6. the vowels.

It has to be supposed that the order of the numerals with the increasing number of strokes from right to left indicate the relative frequency and, therefore, the relative importance of the specific syllables at the isolating-agglutinative stage of Indus. The most frequently used syllables have been placed at the first position and the least used syllables occupy the last position in each series. Because this was the basis of the positioning of the syllables, the uniformity in the places of utterance of the syllables in each series has been guillotined.

As a rule, p d n l are the mostly used sounds, followed by k ḍ ṇ r, t g ṅ v, ṭ b y m, and c j ñ h groups in lesser frequencies, even though the extant texts do not always support it. We can vaguely say, subject to the specific exceptions noted above, that the dentals were the most popular among the stops, followed by cerebrals, gutturals, palatals and labials, though p and k unusually outnumber t ṭ c among the voiceless unaspirates. Coming to Sanskrit, the situation was remarkably changed: the cerebrals were reduced to hopeless minority, the dentals, gutturals, palatals and labials showing the superior presence.

In the first series, we have the voiceless fricatives, very fairly represented, h̲ and ṣ more extensively. The dental s has a lesser presence than ṣ, though the palatal ś is better represented. The Sanskrit school put the cerebral ṣ in the middle of the sibilants in accordance with the positioning of the voiceless stops: ch ṭh th - c ṭ t.

In the second series, we have the voiceless stops, the sequence showing that the unaspirates are more numerous than the aspirates. Among the voiceless unaspirates, p and k have been marked with smaller size, showing their remarkable presence in the language. Then t ṭ c are comparatively low in number. In Sanskrit the situation has completely changed in respect of ṭ, which is utterly in minority. The aspirates too have deplorable presence, ch and kh almost not represented in Indus. The voiceless aspirates may be said to have improved their presence in Sanskrit.

In the third series, we have the voiced stops which, though less numerous than the corresponding voiceless stops, maintain a good proportion of unaspirates and aspirates. In Sanskrit, the cerebrals have drastically suffered.

The fourth series belongs to nasals. Here the surprising fact is the absence of m, which is a dominant sound in Sanskrit. The absence of ṅ does not surprise us, because it never occurs initially in Sanskrit. Perhaps m has been signed slightly differently, , with a number of variants, which perhaps represent m with different vowels.

The fifth series forms a group of heterogenous consonants, the lateral l, the trilled r, the semivowels y and v, and the voiced breathing h. Though the extant texts do not attest the proportion, that should be taken for granted. The situation has changed in Sanskrit. Due to a tendency of rhotacism, r had outnumbered l in Vedic, but just afterwards there was a revival of l which ousted r in Māgadhī.

The real semivowels are y and v, which interchange with i and u. But after the origin or ṛ from r and l at the inflexional stage of Indus, even r and l were considered semivowels due to their interchange with ṛ (and ḷ).

By the time of the RV, the two h of Indus were normalised, though its distinction was maintained in Santhal and Hittite. The RV-Prātiśākhya knew the voiceless h, which it prescribed to avoid in pronunciation.

The vowels have been listed last of all, numerically not all represented too. They had not fully developed as distinct sounds. Therefore, they were called svara (inarticulate sound) later, in contrast with the consonants, called vyañjana (articulate sound) later. The vowel u was the most conspicuous of them, placed at the first position, followed by i and o, others missing till āu with seven strokes appeared.

The situation was drastically changed in Sanskrit, where a had become the dominant vowel at all positions in a word. The Sanskrit school made a drastic revision in the order of the vowels, for which Pāṇini even apologised by highlighting u (1, 2, 27).

This ur-Māheśvarasūtras-order of syllables is the parent of the IE numerals from 5 to 10:

1. ẖa-p-ta = 7
2. ẖa-ṣ-ṭa = 8
3. na-va = 9
4. da-jha = 10
5. pa-ñ-ca = 5
6. ṣa (3) ṣa (3) = 6

Some glaring facts have to be brought into notice in this connection:

The soft breathing h and the hard breathing ẖ were clearly distinguished in the Indus syllabary, both put at the two ends of the consonants. They were normalised as voiced h in Vedic and lost elsewhere. But they continued as voiced and vouceless h in Santhal and Hittite.

The cerebrals are as much native to Sanskrit as all other consonants, which have no place in the IE reconstruction. The reconstructed IE is the parent of the languages west of West-Asia.

Whatever the evidence of archaeology, the Indus inscriptions go to a hoary past, milleniums ago.

Notes and References

1. There are seven syllables from h̲a to ta via pa. Later h̲ turnėd up as s, except in Iranian.
2. There are eight syllables from h̲a to ṭa via ṣa. Later h̲ was lost in all dialects except Iranian, there being hašt in modern Persian.
3. The syllables from na to va are nine only when the nasals are counted six including the unwritten anusvāra.
4. There are ten syllables from da to jha. But/jh/was dialectally pronounced as stop or affricate. Through its affricate value /dzh/, it was deaspirated and reduced to z and then devoiced to ś (Vedic : daśa). Elsewhere, it was gutturalised, devoiced and deaspirated to k.
5. There are five syllables from pa to ca. In the middle the fifth nasal from the right was inserted (Vedic : pañca). The affricate value of /c/ is evident in the Gk pente.
6. Because ṣa heads a group of three sibilants, ṣaṣa (3+3) = 6. (Vedic : ṣaṣ).

   It is clear, all the IE reconstructions for these numerals are purely hypothetical.

12

The Field-symbols of the Indus Texts

Not only the language of the Indus texts, even the field symbols are equally intriguing. As a matter of fact, the field symbols exactly correspond to the language in obscurity.

1. Only the understanding of the one may reveal the mystery of the other. But both have been equally hard to crack.

The brevity of the texts of the Indus inscriptions has led some researchers to assume that it is not a language at all.

2. Others try to read the texts logographically.

3. Some others just take pride in dismissing any solution outright without proposing anything better.

4. And, lastly, some others have gone to the extent of saying that these inscriptions cannot be deciphered at all.

5. But, in spite of that, there are two schools : one holds the view that the language is Dravidian; the other holds that it is some form of Sanskrit.

By Dravidian, it is conceived to be a proto - or common Dravidian, which is not demonstratable even in a reconstructed form. The brevity of the texts has inspired some to see in them the language of the sūtra literature.

6. In other words, they see the inflexional Sanskṛit in them. That is to say, one sees it as agglutinative, the other as inflexional.

The very idea of Sanskrit or Dravidian has inspired the respective scholars to dive into the Vedic Nighaṇṭu and the Dravidian etymological dictionary.

7. A sophisticated language like Sanskrit or Dravidian in the most primitive form of the society is difficult to conceive, though it is also logically contested that society having an urban culture with so excellent achievements cannot be said to be linguistically primitive.

Some think that the monosyllabic words and the absence of grammar in case of the language of the Indus society is incongruous. But it is difficult to measure the linguistic competence of a community corresponding to its social advancement. The most wonderful scientific developments are taking place now when all the languages of the world are in analytic state, generally employing monosyllabic words with as little grammar as possible.

There appears to be a clash among different disciplines: anthropology, archaeology and linguistics, all of them being very young. The ancient discipline of astronomy is always kept outside the present discussion. But if we can think of a primitive form of the human society, why can we not think of the primitive form of language, which is essentially a human affair? Why should linguistic Darwinism be scoffed at?

In respect of a language, we can imagine probably three extremes:

no morphology	:	the most complex morphology
monosyllabic words	:	polysyllabic words
one-word clause	:	many-word clause.

If Sanskrit was perfect, copious and exquisitely refined according to William Jones, it should have started with its imperfect, brief and rugged form, which characterises the Indus texts. The reconstructed IE is made to be the earlier form of Sanskrit, which is an obvious forgery, because it blatantly ignores the principles of the linguistic embryology. A language does not develop in the way the IE has been reconstructed.

To any scholar seeing the Indus texts for the first time, this language appears to have no grammar and just one, two or three monosyllabic words making a clause. Naturally, it should be the most primitive form of a language. When the babbling of the caveman had turned into articulate human sounds, there would have been vowels not more (rather, a few less) than what we see in the diagram of the cardinal vowels. As regards consonants, they should not have been more than what are presented in the syllabic order of the Māheśvarasūtras, where just five places of utterance are involved. This is just a presumption, however.

The vowels would have been the basis of the pronouns, which was perhaps the first part of speech to emerge. The nameless objects were indicated by vowels, meaning just 'this' or 'that'. The consonants were the verbs. Thus it is presumed that the Indus texts containing single signs would have been consonants for verbs. They cannot be vowels. This may be the first step towards decipherment, because at least vowels and consonants have been distinguished.

A primitive man saw everything in the form of an action. He saw a turtle and called it ka, meaning 'moves slowly'. He saw a river and called it na, meaning 'flows'. He even reinforced this idea by extending it as na-da, meaning 'flows (and) makes indistinct noise'. This was the first stage in the evolution of a language, a human speech.

Later, nouns were born from the verbs. Then ka also indicated the object 'moving slowly', namely the 'turtle' itself. Even na-da referred to a 'small river' flowing with indistinct noise. Perhaps adjectives arose simultaneously. As in the primitive form of the human society, the same man was a priest, a warrior, a farmer and a public servant, the same syllable stood for any part of speech.

It was a time when the river later called Sarasvatī in the RV was known just as a clause 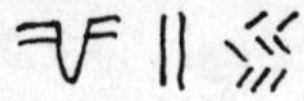 ṣa ra ṣa 'from the nipple flows (and) stops (at the sea). It was a time much beyond the imagination of a historian or archaeologist.

Some of the signs used singly represent the consonant for a verb, even though all of them cannot be individually identified with some idea. However,  ṣ-ṭha may be supposed to stand for 'stop',  ṭha for 'turn',  ra for 'go',  na for 'no',  ni for 'in', and so on. Some other doubtful signs are the following: 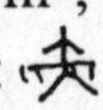 tra 'help, help',  hau 'stop' (to an animal),  ka 'water',  ta 'yes', etc. The question why a small sign was put on a small piece of clay is baffling. It may be supposed that they were put behind a magnifying glass to indicate the signal clearly, as we see in the traffic control system today.

Then we come to the bisyllabic texts. These too convey some kind of information to the people on a public place. The Dholavira sign-board text gives a long message in many little clauses. Naturally, they are the most primitive form of clauses, generally subject + verb, rarely verb + oblique case (when the subject was known from the context). A three-sign text consists of subject + object + verb or oblique case + subject + verb, etc.. The verb preceding the object made a passive clause.

Many texts are accompanied by field-symbols. Though no possible connection between the inscription and associated field symbol has been found, it has been observed that the same text appears with different field symbols, and vice versa. If the same field symbol is associated with several texts, the field symbol may point to some specific context, some department or specialised field of work of the society. This may be the primitive way of chaptering a book.

If the same text has several field symbols, the text may be supposed to differ in meaning in every new context. That is to say, the field symbols may change the meaning of the text. The field symbols may even indicate present, past or future tense. Then the largest occurrence of the field symbol may indicate the most usual tense, probably the past which, usually shown by the prefix ā, is not seen in writing. As a rule, the tense-mechanism is visible only in respect of future, expressed by gha, in the extant texts.

The text 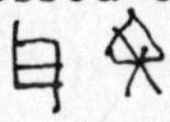 ṇa ga seems to say: the light went away = the darkness came. The field symbol 'unicorn facing a cult object' seems to indicate that the animals were fed at night so that they could be harnessed the next day for work. Even today in the Indian villages every householder has troughs for the milch animal and oxes, called nādī, and the fodder put in it is called sānī. These words are very ancient.

The text  ṣa ṭha seems to say: the egg rolled forth. But the field symbol associated with it is uncertain: 'serpent (?) entwined around a pillar'. The 'rolling' of the text reflects in the 'entwining' of the symbol, but nothing can be said any further.

We may presume that the field symbols are the broad contexts or chapters of the Indus texts. One may help in the interpretation of the other. In Mīmāṃsā, abhāva (absence) is a pramāṇa or source of knowledge. The absence of the possibly existing 'horse' in the Indus pictographs too has some context. The meanings of these field symbols may be sought in the enigmatic hymns and individual stanzas of the RV, specially of the 10th maṇḍala.

With the same text 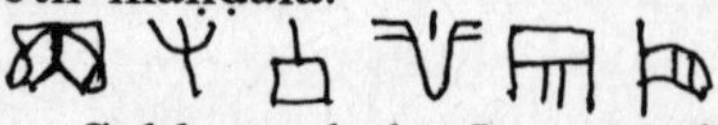 ra bī ṣu va ṇa ṭha, there are two field symbols. In one, there is 'a man armed with a sickle-shaped weapon facing a seated woman with dishevelled hair and upraised arms'. In the other, there is 's nude female figure upside down with thighs drawn apart and a crab (?) issuing from her womb; two tigers standing face to face rearing on their hindlegs'. (Mahadevan).

Because there are two clauses in the text, each field symbol has two parts. Two field symbols related with the same text indicate that the context may be different in which case the same text may have different meanings. The lady with the dishevelled hair may point to 'raising alarm' and the armed man may indicate the 'rescue operation'. The same text with the other field symbol may have a different meaning.

Similarly, in case of the same context (field symbol) the two texts may indicate similar situation. Just as we have more ideas in our mind than there are words in our language, there are more texts than contexts in Indus.

They are like different chapters in a book, the various departments of public works in the society. Let us further examine this view about the field symbols.

13

The Symbolism of the Indus Inscriptions

On account of some peculiar features of the Indus texts, one is liable to make a number of debatable speculations. The peculiar features are the following: 1. The texts are very small; there are even one-sign texts; generally there are two-sign and three-sign texts; and some texts are even longer. 2. They have been inscribed on small clay-tablets, later baked in fire or dried in sun. There are also copper tablets, bronze implements, ivory or bone rods on which the texts have been written. 3. There are peculiar field symbols accompanying most of the texts.

If these features are put in the form of questions, they are liable to be very embarrassing and not easy to answer. Every answer may be highly speculative. But this is the way we can proceed to solve the problem.

It appears to represent the earliest form of the human speech. It is just on the border of babbling of the caveman turning into articulate human sounds. Each sound is of the nature of a syllable of the CV (consonant-vowel) type. It was not the time for VC or CVC type of syllables. Such types were unknown even to Prakrits.

It is difficult to measure the time in this process. Every step would have consumed a long stretch of time. The evolution of writing would have been the affairs of a whole millenium.

If it was an utterance of the one syllable, it was the verb. If there was, e.g. na, it meant 'it flows', pointing to a flowing river. Even if it was extended by -da, na-da just meant 'flows (and) makes indistinct noise'. That is so say, an object was nameless at that time. Any object could be indicated through 'action' (verb).

But, we suppose, a time came when the verb itself turned into a noun through the adjectival meaning. That is to say, na 'flows' turned into 'the (flowing) river', and thus the noun was born. The birth of a noun initiated the formation of the first clause: subject + verb. There was :ṇa ra = A creature goes; ṇa ga = The light has gone. Because it was the beginning of a language, the context showed whether it was present or past. A group of three syllables or monosyllabic words comprised subject (s) + object (o) + verb (v). In the first stage of the language, the isolating stage as it is called, the manipulation of the 'order' of words made various types of clauses. Thus: ṇa ma ṣa (s+o+v) = The knowledge produces happiness; ta na ṣa (oblique case + s + v) = From the womb gems come out; ṣa ra ṣa (oblique case + v + v) = From the nipple (mountain) flows (and) ends (at the sea), etc. There was also gā va (oblique case + v) = Goes into the pen. And so on.

Thus the smallness of the Indus texts has made us speculate on the early form of the human speech. But it is not just speculation. We know, these clauses did not stop at that point of their origin. They travelled a long distance. The clauses noted above had turned up as phrases with the same body of syllables; ṇara = a walking creature, ṇaga = the vanishing light, gāva = going into the pen, etc. This was the early phase of the next or the agglutinative stage of the language, when bisyllabic and longer words began to be formed. Then it was not possible to repeat the word to form pl. The pl forms began to be made by means of the affix -ṣa: ṇara-ṣa, gāva-ṣa, etc. Corresponding to the subject, even the verb became pl. by means of the same affix, besides being prefixed with ā for the past tense Thus : ha (say) present : ā-ha (past-say = said) past : ā-hu-ṣa (past-say pl.), etc. It was followed by the affix for the present tense and the distinction of person and number.

At the third or the inflexional stage, these clauses were drastically reduced phonetically with frog's jump in meaning: nár (a creature, a man), nág (night), tánas (offspring), etc. The pl. forms gāvaṣa, ṇaraṣa, āhuṣa, etc. too were reduced as gāvas, náras, āhús, etc. Then they were analysed in a different way by the new grammarians. These forms are attested through the Vedic language.

From the allegory of the Vāmana-incarnation of Viṣṇu, we can imagine the early form of the Vedic language. The language of the Indus inscriptions represents the Vāmana-incarnation and the Vedic language represents the Kṛṣṇa-incarnation of Viṣṇu.

The speculation regarding the second feature of the texts may be more embarrassing. The Indus society ultimately developed an urban and technically advanced culture. There was an excellent town-planning. There was drainage system for sewage and rain-water. The streets were laid out in an efficient grid pattern. As far as we have read and understood the texts, these archaeological facts are coded in the inscriptions.

When the writing had started, the Indus culture was at the height of perfection, even though the language lay just at the isolating stage, slowly moving towards the agglutinative stage.

The monosyllabic texts were various signals; e.g. ra was a signal for 'go', ṣṭha for 'stop', ṭha for 'turn', na for 'in', etc. Perhaps these little syllables were put before lighted magnifying glass to control the traffic on the cross-roads and to serve as sign-boards at the entrance of important public places.

A text appears to be read : bu jña ṣu ḍho ṣa. The meaning perhaps is : if the water is contaminated, flush it out. It is suggested by a siphoning instrument nowadays in the countryside, called ḍhos. Another text, with a different clause in the second part, reads : bu jña ṣu ma ṇu ṣa . It seems to mean : if the water is contaminated, the death is certain. We now realise that mánus (a man) is not 'one who thinks' from 'man' (to think), but 'one who is destined to die'. The indus texts make us wiser even linguistically, because all Vedic words are not derived from the Vedic roots. The Indus clauses are very small, often thwarting the very idea of their representing a language, but they have been paraphrased in the RV. A very small text ṣa ṭha (the egg rolled) has been paraphrased thus : hiraṇya-garbhaḥ sam-avartatāgre (a golden egg rolled forth in the beginning). These samples of the texts show that though the clauses are so small, they represent the grandmother of the long Vedic verses or hemistichs.

Their inscribing on clay- and copper-tablets, etc. indicate that they were meant for public places, probably put behind magnifying glasses to be read clearly. There should have been even long texts on perishable material, but they have been destroyed by nature during this long period.

The peculiar field symbols of the texts are the most embarrassing features. But as we gradually comprehend the texts, the mystery of the field symbols seems to be resolved. The field symbols have two aspects : 1. There is the same field symbol associated with several texts. 2. On the other hand, there is the same text associated with more than one field symbol.

The same field symbol accompanying several texts appears like the title of a book having several chapters. The unicorn is the most important symbol, perhaps being the main occupation of the Indus society. As a rule, the symbolism of the field symbols may be sought in the enigmatic stanzas of the RV. The good wishes expressed in the last hymn of the RV (10,191) may have their inspiration from the texts and field symbols of the Indus inscriptions. The unicorn represents the idea 'samāna' (equal, same).

samāno mantraḥ samitiḥ samānī
samānaṃ manaḥ saha cittam eṣām,
samānaṃ mantram abhi mantraye vaḥ
samānena vo haviṣā juhomi.
samānī va ākutiḥ samānā hṛdayāni vaḥ,
samānam astu vo mano yathā susahāsati.

Some scholars see the unity of the heterogenous cultures and of the ideologically different social groups in the mixed figures of the animals. The absence of the 'horse' on the seals has been greatly highlighted. Because abhāva (absence) is a pramāṇa in mīmāṃsā, the absence of the horse figures on the Indus seals indicates its presence with specific qualification. In the Pauranic mythology, every Hindu god has been assigned a conveyance, beginning from the rat to elephant, but the 'horse' has been assigned to no god. We cannot, on this ground, say that the pauranic people did not know any horse.

One field symbol in relation to several texts of the inscriptions is nothing less than one book having several chapters, though it is difficult to name the book or its title.

When there are two field symbols associated with the same text, the meaning of the latter appears to differ according to the context. Here the field symbol indicates the different contexts of the same text.

For example, the text ra bī ṣu va ṇa ṭha has two field symbols:

1. a man armed with a sickle-shaped weapon facing a seated a woman dishevelled hair and unraised arms.
2. a nude female upside down with thighs drawn apart and a crab (?) issuing from the womb, two tigers standing face to face rearing on their hindlegs.

-Mahadevan.

The meaning of the same texts must differ as suggested by the second clause va ṇa ṭha evolving in Vedic as vanád (fire) RV 2,4,5 and as the verb vart (vṛt) 'to roll'.

It appears hard to believe that the Vedic gods were the administrative officers of the urban Indus culture.

Agni, a gni in the clause form, means: he enlightens. He was the officer in charge of the enlightenment in various forms. He was also probably the Priminister.

Indra, i nda ra in the clause form, means: he brightens the darkness, drives away the enemies.

Rudra, ru da ra in the clause form, means; the fire burns the evil . The word is still trisyllabic in the RV. He was the most ruthless security officer and inflicted severe punishment on the offenders. He wore the most gorgeous dresses.

Viṣṇu, vi ṣṇu in the clause form, means; surveys the

space. He was the land survey officer and the townplanner of the Indus society.

The other Vedic gods belong to a period when the Indus culture was gradually merging with the Vedic culture, because they appear to have been derived from the Vedic roots.

It is time for us to examine these speculations. Our linguistic Darwinism has brought about the meeting of the grand-daughter Vedic with the grandmother, the isolating stage of the same, called Indus or Sarasvatī. The inscribing of the texts on clay-tablets and bone-rods may indicate the unavailability of the modern facilities, but they must have also thought of the durability of the written documents. For a penetrating enquiry into the field symbols we have to explore the enigmatic hymns and stanzas of the RV. Just as we have found the grandmother of the Vedic language engraved in the ruins of the Indus valley, we may find the symbols explained in those enigmas.

14

On the Absence of 'Horse' on the Indus Seals

In the mīmāṃsā system of philosophy, abhāva (absence) is a pramāṇa (a source of knowledge).

In the Indian mythology, almost all gods have some animals for their conveyance; e.g. Viṣṇu rides on Garuḍa, Siva on a bull, Durgā on a lion, Sarasvatī on a swan, Yama on a buffalo, Indra on the elephant Airāvata, and so on. Even the war-god Skanda has a peacock as his conveyance. The horse has not been assigned to any god as his conveyance. But, on this ground, we cannot say that the horse was unknown to these people.

This abhāva (absence) of the horse in the Hindu's list of the conveyances of the gods justifies the absence of the horse on the Indus seals. Perhaps the indecent behaviour of this animal was detested even in the Indian prehistory, and this tradition of not highlighting horses as animal had continued till the Purāṇic age.

Though the IE word aśva for this animal did not continue in the later age, ghoṭa is a pan-Indian name of this animal in all the dialects. This ghoṭa is a word of agglutinative formation : gho- is the same element as we have in gho-ra (terrible), gho-ṣa (loudnoise), etc. In the colloquial language ṭa means 'foot, leg'. Thus ghoṭa means an animal 'having injurious hind-leg', and in this sense it is not different from aśva (an injurious and strong animal), as we shall just see.

In the traditional Sanskrit lexicons, which is supposed to preserve the monosyllabic words of the isolating stage of some prehistoric primitive language, ha means 'a horse'. As a matter of fact, ha (which is voiceless out of the two h-sounds of Indus, quoted verbatim in the Māheśvarasūtras of the Pāṇini's grammar) itself has been variously extended : by śa (injury) and va (strength) in Vedic, where h itself was lost, making a-ś-va (an injurious and strong animal); by ra (speed) and va (strength), where too h was lost, making arvā (a fast-running strong animal); by śa-pha (injurious hoofs) in Iranian, where too h was lost, making *aspha deaspirated as aspa; by -kva in Latin, finally evolving as equus (also losing the initial h); by -pva in Greek hippos and by -rsa in Germanic *hors (where h has been retained). Even the Vedic *ha-r-va was added to gand- (the same element as we have in garda -bha 'ass'), making gandharva, meaning probably 'an assed horse', a mixed breed. As the original ha (horse) migrated to the western countries, every time its breed was improved and got a new name.

Perhaps also because of the mixed genesis of this animal, it was not deemed proper to pictograph it on the Indus seals. It was not only the people but even the horse which had migrated to the western countries.

15

The Urban and the Pastoral Cultures

We know that the Indus society was urban and the Vedic society was pastoral, but a natural catastrophe like fire, flood or earthquake must have intervened to bring a drastic change.

A few Indus texts which have been provisionally read appear to suggest how the urban culture was transformed into the pastoral Vedic culture. For example :

	Text No.	*Reads*
1.	2420	ru i yū ṣi na ṣa ra
2.	2355	bu jña ṣu ḍho ṣa
3.	4304	ra bǐ ṣu va ṇa ṭha
4.	4237	ra cǐ ṣa
5.	5086	ra jǐ ṣu ni ṣa ra

The reading is unilateral to the extent that it is based partially on the syllabic order of the Māheśvarasūtras of the Pāṇini's grammar, reflecting in the specific shapes and lengths of the Indus numeral script. The interpretations of the syllables thus read are also unilateral, based on the authority of the traditional Sanskrit lexicons of the monosyllabic words. Both the tools of reading and interpretation, though not extremely weak, have little respect among the scholars. They are like the bones of an ass appearing as those of a horse, or vice versa, to an archaeologist.

The clause ḍho ṣa of the second text seems to reflect in dhos, a siphoning instrument of the countryside in India today. On this basis, the Indus text means : If the drainage waters (bū) become contaminated (jña ṣu), siphon it out (dho ṣa). Whatever the urban form of the present dhos, it is still continuing in India, showing the continuation of the Indus culture till today.

The third text reads ra bī ṣu va ṇa ṭha, which means : When the fire heats the water, in the dwelling (va) vapour (ṇa) circulates (ṭha). The first clause seems to reflect in the Vedic ṛbīsa (a chasm, abyas from which hot vapours arise). In the RV, it is a vapourised chamber from which Atri was rescued by Aśvins. As a matter of fact, the RV describes the incidents of the urban Indus culture where the fireman Atri (or his family) was rescued by the fire-brigade operated by the Aśvins of the rapid action force. The Aśvins were those who were quick in action (āśu = quick). The Atris, the firemen of the urban culture became the fire-priest of the pastoral culture. Later ṛbīsa refers to that abyss in which fruits are matured, as even now in the countryside. This ṛbīsa has now taken the form of borsi in which the fire is stored to warm the room in the countryside in winter.

Then it appears that rabīsa was a 'centrally heated room' in the urban Indus culture which could become dangerously suffocating. We can imagine the gradual transformation of the urban facilities in the pastoral society.

The fourth clause reads ra cī ṣa (the fire produces heat). We cannot say whether it refers to a 'blast furnace' in the urban Indus society, but later its fossilised form ṛcīṣa means a 'frying pan', which intervenes the fire and its heat. Perhaps the 'frying pan' is the pastoral form of some scientific apparatus.

The last text is the most important. The first three signs for ra jī ṣu and the last three signs for ni ṣa ra make two clauses, syntactically related: Because the fire produces energy, in the interior (ni) the speed is caused (ṣa ra, passively for ra ṣa) The whole text seems to refer to the operation of a steam-engine. Both these clauses appear to reflect in the Vedic vocables, ṛjīṣa RV and nisara VS. The former qualifies Indra, who may be 'fiery' energetic, speedy', and the latter is entangled in some obscure equation :

for manyu- (anger) : there is ayas-tāpa (iron-smith)
for krodha- (id) : nisara (?????)

The equation can be solved by taking nisara to be a similar professional who, according to the context, may be a 'steam-engineer' Thus, literally, nisara is a 'steam-engineer', who may have become 'controller' of anger in the Vedic context.

Thus we see that an urban society can peacefully march into the pastoral society, where a 'centrally heated room' becomes an 'abyss', a 'steam-engineer' becomes a 'solicitor', and so on. However, the cause of this transition may be generally tragic.

16

The Main Food of the Indus People

If the sign  of the Indus script represents the syllable gau, we may be able to say that the 'wheat' is native to India and not an import from the central Asia. It was the main food of the people of the Indus valley civilisation, apart from yava 'barley' and vrīhi 'rice'.

The Sanskrit lexicons of the monosyllabic words have ya for 'barley', the first syllable in the formation of yava. Because yava is just the 'corn' in general in Avesta, ya at the isolating stage of Indus should have been 'corn' in general.

The bisyllabic yava would have emerged at the agglutinative stage initially as a phrase, then as a lexical item. At the isolating stage, ya va would have existed in the form of a clause, meaning 'the corn (of the particular type) strengthens (the body), because va means 'strong' in the traditional lexicons. Though each corn would have been distinguished by the specific syllable at the isolating stage, it was at the agglutinative stage that the corn was distinguished through specific quality.

About vrīhi, also a clause at the isolating stage, nothing can be said beyond the fact that it was 'a summer crop through plenty of rain', suggested by va for 'water', rī for 'heat' + hi for 'cause', meaning : produced through water in summer.

The first two syllables of godhūma 'wheat' occur in the modern Dravidian languages : Kannad gōdi, Tamil kōti. Perhaps at this stage of the formation of this word, or slightly earlier, the Indus community had disintegrated in several groups. The second syllable of godhūma is the same as dhū in Hindi dhūp 'the heat of the sun'. The colloquial dhīp 'to be hot' and other dh-syllables as in dhūma 'smoke', etc. are coming down from the isolating and agglutinative stages of Indus. Perhaps the second syllable had begun to differ at this stage as shown by *dhi in Dravidian and dhū in Vedic. Perhaps godhu/dhi means 'the wheat heats (the body). Both the final vowels were used dialectally in the Indus society. We may not be surprised if the second syllable had even a different consonant in some other dialects.

Because the Avesta has the trisyllabic gantuma, ma was added to godhu- in the western and northern dialects at the inflexional stage, while the southern and eastern dialects limped at the agglutinative stage. The word godhūma could have meant : the corn is enjoyable.

Because the words of the Dravidian languages are identical with the Vedic words just at the first, and rarely upto the second syllable, their relationship is doubted or even rejected. We have only to draw the conclusion that the separation took place at the very early stage of the mother language.

It is due to this that the syllabic group gau dhū ma cannot be traced in the Indus inscriptions. The Indus was a developing language : there was only gau at the isolating stage; it was extended as gau dhū ạt the agglutinative stage; and it was finally extended as godhūma at the inflexional stage.

The Dravidian and Munda groups of languages marked time at the second syllable and underwent further phonetic change, as in Tamil kōti.

If we have to consider the cognateness of words among the Vedic, Dravidian and Munda languages, we should restrict the identity of syllables upto the first and second. Later each language has developed in its own way.

Notes and References

1. Cf. gantumo yavānam ratufriš 'among the corns the wheat is agreeable to Ratu'.
2. We are inspired to propose it because the final vowel is -i instead of the expected u. Had the Dravidian group separated a little later, it would have been dhū at the second syllable.
3. Though the first syllable is deaspirated in the Vedic dadhikrā 'the rolling ball of the morning sun', there is the reduplicated dh in the Indus text no. 4320 dha dhe gra ṣa gha 'the brightly hot sun will appear'.
4. The adjective ratu-friš 'agreeable to Ratu' is remarkable.
5. It may be supposed that godhu, a phrase meaning 'the energetic corn' was restricted to 'wheat' in meaning and made a clause godhuma meaning 'the wheat ripened', which contracted as godhūma 'wheat' at the inflexional stage. (cf. tata maha 'the father has grown old' : tatāmaha 'grandfather').

17

SRI AUROBINDO

On the Common Origin of the Indian Languages

It was perhaps in the last years of his writings that Sri Aurobindo had expressed his views on the origin of the Aryan speech. (The secret of the Vedas, the last chapter). He began with his criticism of the IE reconstruction, e.g., of patēr for pitár, patēr, father, Vater, etc., which was just spreading a blanket over the cognate forms. It is surprising that, once this sort of reconstruction was started, it was never challenged, though the individual sounds were variously modified to suit the ablaut relationships in the cognate languages; cf., e.g., the earliest 'avis akvasas ka' and the latest 'owis ekwos que'.

After examining the controversial grounds for the relationship of languages, Sri Aurobindo stated that the origin of languages should be governed by natural laws. That is to say, there should be a science of linguistic embryology to explain the origin of words, just as in case of the origin of species. Thus he conceived that if pitár, patēr, etc. were cognates, the seed is just p-. It was, first of all, extended by the cardinal vowels a i u e o, short and long.

Thus a single p- emerged as pa, pā, pi, etc. The simple p could also have been extended by another consonant from either side (rp or pr), which could take all the vowels. He further says that though all the syllables formed in this way could not endure, those which did left a vigorous progeny behind them, which preserve in themselves the evidence for the existence of their progenitor. A large number of monosyllabic words, that is, bare syllables like ka, kha, etc. have been handed down to us through the traditional Sanskrit lexicons.

That is to say, at the earliest stage of the origin of human speech, only monosyllabic words had appeared in the language. In other words, each syllable was a word in the beginning of the origin of a language. But Sri Aurobindo does not say anything more on the fate of these monosyllabic words, which were nouns, pronouns, adjectives and verbs at the same time, just as each man in the primitive constitution of the human society fulfilled at once several functions.

How each syllable was capable of numerous different meanings and each idea could be expressed by many syllables arose inevitably out of the very nature of the human speech in its beginning. A certain object was expressed by a certain sound because of some striking characteristics conceived by the early human thinking.

At the earliest stage of the evolution of human speech, the initial conception was that of an action or verb. If something was mentioned, it was indicated by a verb; e.g., pointing to a river, na meant 'it flows'. Gradually, the verb became a noun. If some additional idea was added, namely 'it flows and makes indistinct noise', it was extended by da, making na-da. Gradually, nada or f. nadī also referred to the river. It was much later that the root nad (avyakte śabde) was deduced from this noun. In this way, each sound was attached with some object or idea, and also vice versa.

Perhaps the vowels were restricted for indicating an object without a name, and later they became bases for the pronouns.

After this stage of the monosyllabic and bisyllabic clauses, there was the beginning of a new pattern : subject + verb, accompanied by some extensions and manipulations, namely : subject + object + verb, oblique-case + subject + verb, oblique-case + verb, and so on. Perhaps this was the climax of the socalled isolating stage.

If we look at the texts of the Indus inscriptions, we feel that all the characteristics of an isolating language are found in them. Thus the language of the Indus inscriptions represents the earliest human speech. This is just based on the graphic form of the inscriptions, without reading the texts.

If we try to read the texts of the Indus inscriptions, specially some two-sign and three-sign texts, the immediate help we receive is from the traditional Sanskrit lexicons. Some of the syllabes of the Sanskrit alphabet, as compiled in the traditional Sanskrit lexicons, refer to animals, birds, insects and physical objects, and some of them are portrayed in the Indus script, namely : turtle  ka, mountain 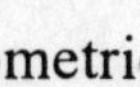 da, fish 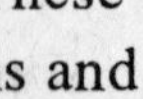 na, leaf  pa, spider 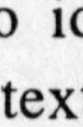 ba, bee  bha, etc.

A later help has come from the Indus numerals of various shapes and sizes being identified with the syllabic order of the Māheśvarasūtras of the Pāṇini's grammar.

These two have combined to identify the geometrical signs and enabled to read a few texts with confidence. The first text to be read was 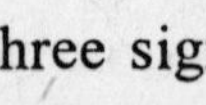 ta na ṣa. It had at least three more duplicates, that is : .  . . Thus three signs for each of ta, na and ṣa were recognised : ta 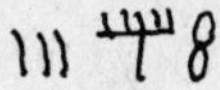 na 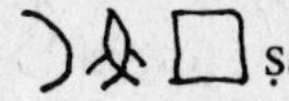 ṣa 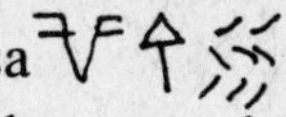

In this way, a good number of texts have been read :

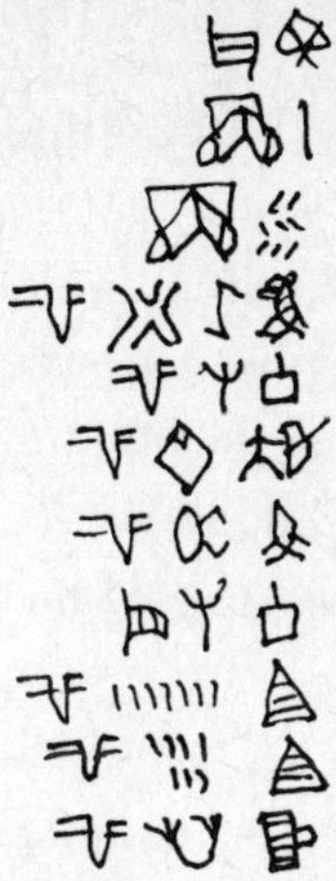

ṇa ga
la ṭha
ṣa ṭha
śa ma yo ṣa
va ṇa ṣa
rau ci ṣa
na bha ṣa
va ṇa ra
h̲a ṭha ṣa
h̲a ḍha ṣa
rāu ka ṣa

These texts of the Indus inscriptions appear to reflect in the rare vocables of the RV :

ṇa ga	:	nág 'night'
la ṭha	:	ṛtá 'order of the universe'
ṣa ṭha	:	sát 'the rolling egg'
śa ma yo ṣa	:	śám yós 'wellbeing and welfare'
va ṇa ṣa	:	vánas in vanas-pati 'plant'
rau ci ṣa	:	rócis 'light'
na bha ṣa	:	nábhas 'sky'
va ṇa ra	:	vánar in vanar-gû, -ṣád
h̲a ṭha ṣa	:	satás in sató-vīra, -mahat, -bṛhat
h̲a ḍha ṣa	:	sadhá
rau ka ṣa	:	rókas 'light'

In the centre of the Indus clauses and the reduced, wornout and mutilated vocables of the RV, there were certainly the phrases at the intermediate stage which have gone unrecorded. That is to say, between the Indus clause ṇa ga and the Vedic vocable nág, there was a phrase *naga with appropriate meaning. Even some verbs of the isolating stage have come down to Vedic as enclitics; e.g. ha, hi, tu, ca, etc.

On the basis of the meanings of the vocables of the RV, the texts of the Indus inscriptions have been interpreted in the following way :

ṇa ga (light movement) = The light is going away.
la ṭha (time circle) = The time turns round.
ṣa ṭha (embryo circle) = The egg rolled.
śa ma yo ṣa (evil end comfort embryo)
= Let evil end; let comfort come.
va ṇa ṣa (water life embryo)
= From the water life comes.
rau ci ṣa (fire light embryo)
= From the fire there is light.
na bha ṣa (emptiness light embryo)
= In the sky there is light.
va ṇa ra (dwelling life speed)
= In the dwelling animals go.
ẖa ṭha ṣa (emptiness disc embryo)
= From the empty space a ball emerged.
ẖa ḍha ṣa (emptiness sound embryo)
= In the empty space there was a big bang.
rau ka ṣa (sun light embryo)
= From the sun there is light.

Sri Aurobindo conceived the Sanskrit syllabary to be the true representative of the syllabary of the earliest Aryan speech, though his views about ṛ l being original vowels and the cerebrals being secondary consonants can be questioned. Also, without taking into account the stage between the isolating and inflexional, he suggested the extension of the primitive syllables, which leaves a lacuna. The polysyllabic forms of the Vedic language are not the results of extensions which he suggested but the result of the simple morphology at the earlier stage. For example, the root nad is the result of its deduction from the noun nada or f. nadī, which made indistinct noise while flowing.

The forward and backward reading and interpretation of the texts establishes the relation between the language of the Indus inscriptions and that of the RV : the former is at the isolating stage, the latter at the inflexional stage; the former is the grandmother of the latter; and the Indus culture lies two stations before the Vedic culture.

If the language of the Indus inscriptions is two stations before the Vedic language, and is the grandmother of the inflexional Vedic, it may be naturally the mother of the agglutinative proto-Dravidian and proto-Munda, which could not reach the inflexional stage. That is why, the modern descendants of the Vedic language, though at the agglutinative stage like Dravidian and Munda dialects, have also some amount of inflexion borrowed from the inflexional ancestor, but the modern Dravidian and Munda dialects have no inflexion worthy of name.

But they all possess the common seed, as noted by Sri Aurobindo. The word for 'father' has p- and that for mother has m-. That is why, Aryan has bāp, Dravidian has appā and Munda has āpā for 'father'. But all of them have colloquially ammā for 'mother', which goes to Vedic ambā. What was prefixed and how at some prehistoric period is a different matter. It was on the basis of these seed-sounds that Sri Aurobindo had promised to show the common origin of all the Indian languages. But he left it for us.

These seed-sounds indicate the separation of the proto-Aryan, Dravidian and Munda at a very early period in the history, several thousand years brfore the emergence of pitar and māter from the same seeds. He asserts that Tamil and Sanskrit differ only due to an early separation of the two groups. The Tamil numerals are early Aryan vocables; e.g. e- in Sanskrit e-ka for one and in Tamil e-lu for seven is the early seed. The absence of a common vocabulary for common ideas is not necessarily a proof of diverse origin. Sri Aurobindo has seen the common origin of Aryan, Munda and Dravidian dialects through his yogic vision at a prehistoric period far beyond the range of our historical imagination.

18

The Evolutionary Syntax in Indus-sanskrit

The original Indus clause-pattern being subject (s) + verb (v), it had expanded as subject (s) + object (o) + verb (v), oblique-case + s + v and s + v + o (passive), as indicated in the inscriptions. It had, later, further undergone some manipulations as the society advanced in culture : The analysis of the popular word gāva for 'cow' shows that it was v + oblique-case. It was also reversed in case of bīja (oblique-case + v). There may have been some more manipulations. The plurality was indicated by repeating the monosyllabic words so many times, and it was also known to the Sanskrit grammarians. This was the isolating stage of the language:

na	=	flows
na da	=	flows and makes indistinct noise.
ṇa ga	=	the light has gone away.
ṇa ma ṣa	=	the knowledge gives happiness.
ta na ṣa	=	from the womb gems come out.
bu ṣa ci	=	from the water is generated the light.
gā va	=	goes into the pen.
bī ja	=	in the water it grows.

ga ga ga ṇa	=	the stars were shining.
dha	=	shines
dha dha	=	shines brightly.

As the Indus language transisted into the agglutinative stage the repetition of words and the manipulaiton of the word-water stopped. Various morphological elements appeared to express various ideas.

They may be briefly mentioned below :

gāva ā-ṣa	=	Cow past-be(there was).
gāva-ṣa ā-ṣu-ṣu	=	Cow-pl. past-be-pl.
ṇara-ṣa ā-hu-ṣa	=	Man-pl, past-say-pl.
tata ma-ha	=	Father time-perfect (has grown old).
mraga ku ca-ra	=	There had been beast on the earth.
dhadhegra go cara	=	The bright sun had been in view.
dha-dha-ti	=	They shine brightly.

At the inflexional stage, the original s + v pattern was extensively expanded, the main kernals of which are detailed below :

Expansion of the verbal concepts

1. s-1 + v-1 (intr.) : putro gacchati, putro hasati.
2. s-2 + s-1 $\rightarrow$ 0 + v-2 (tr. from intr.) : pitā putraṃ gamayati, pitā putraṃ hāsayati
3. s-1 + 0 + v-2 (trans. verb):
   a. putro vedaṃ paṭhati
   b. śiṣya odanaṃ pacati
   c. patnī vanaṃ paśyati
   d. bhṛtyaḥ kaṭaṃ karoti

The causative form of a verb is responsible for the manifestation of various case-forms, accusative, instrumental and even dative, as we may just see.

Manifestation of cases

4. s-2 + s-1 → acc. + 0 + v-3 (causative of the tr. verb):
   pitā putraṃ vedam paṭhayati
5. s-2 + s-1 → instr. + 0 + v-3 :
   guruḥ śiṣyeṇa odanaṃ pācayati
6. dative rājā patnyai vanaṃ darśayati
7. s-3 + s-2 → instr. + s-1 → 0 + v-3 (caus. of the caus. of intr.) : mātā pitrā putaṃ gamayati (preṣayati)

bhṛtyaḥ kaṭaṃ karoti → svāmī bhṛtyena/bhṛtyaṃ kaṭam kārayati

bhṛtya bhāraṃ vahati → svāmī bhṛtyena bhāraṃ vāhayati

vāhā rathaṃ vahanti → sūto vāhān rathaṃ vāhayati

vaṭur annaṃ khādati sa vaṭunā annaṃ khādayati

Climb-down : Reflexive and passive

8. a. trans. verb → reflexive, o → nominative:
   = vanaṃ dṛśyate, āśramo dadṛśe, vrīhiḥ pacyate (no subject)

   b. s-1 → instr + v- passive
   = putreṇa gamyate/hasyate

   c. s-2 → instr. + o → nom.
   + v-2 passive = pitrā putraḥ preṣyate/ hāsyate, putreṇa vedaḥ paṭhyate, śiṣyeṇa odanaḥ pacyate, patnyā vanaṃ dṛśyate

   d. s-2 → instr. + o-2 → nom
   + o-1 acc + v 3-p= pitrā putro vedaṃ pāṭhyate
   (According to tradition, also pitrā putraṃ vedaḥ pāṭhyate: wrong).

   e. s-2 → instr. + o-2 instr

+ o-1 → nom. + v 3-p = guruṇā śiṣyeṇa odanaḥ
pācyate, svāminā bhṛtyena
kaṭah kāryate, svāminā
bhṛtyena bhāro vāhyate,
sūtena vāhai ratho vāhyate

Combinations and reductions

9. (s + o + v) + (s + o + v) = s + o-l + o-2 + v
asau gāṃ dogdhi + asau payo dogdhi = asau gāṃ payo dogdhi
10. Passive of 9:s-instr. + o-l → nom. + o-2 acc. + v-passive = amunā gauḥ payo duhyate
The o-1 is the genuine object of the combined clause, not the o-2, as generally supposed due to proximity with the main verb.
11. (s + o + v) + (s + o + v) = s + o + o +v kṛṣṇas tam uvāva + k. idaṃ vākyam u. = kṛṣṇas tam idaṃ vākyam uvāca
(The first o has the value of the dative, = tasmai 'to him').
12. (s-l + o + v) + (s-2 + o + v) = s-1 + s-2 → instr. + o + v: rāmo rāvaṇaṃ jaghāna+vāṇo r. ja. = rāmo vāṇena rāvaṇaṃ jaghāna
13. (s + v) + (s + v) = s + s (one of them in instr. from) + v: putra āgacchat + pitā āgacchat =putreṇa pitā/ putraḥ pitrā (saha) āgacchat.
14 o + v; if v → non-verb, o → dative : rāmaṃ namāmi, nam namas, rāmam rāmāya : rāmāya namaḥ Similarly, tubhyaṃ svasti, agnaye svāhā, pitṛbhyaḥ svadhā
15. (s + o-1 + v) + (s + o-2 + v) = s + o + v-absolutive + o-2 + v: sa vipram abhi-praiti + sa gāṃ dadāti = sa vipram abhi-pretya gāṃ dadāti

16. Take out abhi-pretya from 15: vipram → viprāya = sa viprāya gāṃ dadāti
17. (s + o + v-future) + (s + v) = s + o + v-infinitive + v: sa phalam āneṣyati + sa gacchati = sa phalam ānetuṃ gacchati
18. Take out ānetum from 17: phalam → phalāya = sa phalāya gacchati
19. Infinitive = verbal noun + dative: yaṣṭum = yāgāya
20. (s + [o] + v) + (s + v) = s + o + v-absolutive + v
    a. sa (odanaṃ) khādati + (tataḥ) sa gacchati = sa (odanaṃ) khāditvā gacchati
    b. sa prāsādam ārohati + sa prekṣate = sa prāsādam āruhya prekṣate
21. Take out absolutive from 20b: accustive → ablative = sa prāsādāt prekṣate
    Similarly, vṛkṣaṃ apetya = vṛkṣāt, coraṃ dṛṣṭvā = corāt, etc.
22. s + o + v-2 : v-2 → v-l, s → ablative, o → nominative: himālayo gaṅgāṃ janayati, janayati → jāyate = himālayād gaṅgā jāyate, pitā putram adhyāpayati : adhyāpayati → adhīte: pituḥ putro'dhīte
23. s + v : v → verbal noun, s → genitive, kālidāsaḥ karoti : karoti kṛti, kriyā, karman: kālidāsasya kṛtiḥ s + o + v : v → verbal noun, o → genittive, s → instumental kālidāsaḥ kāyaṃ karoti : kālidāsena kāvyasya kṛtiḥ
24. (s + v understood) + (s + v) = s-locative + s + v: tvaṃ nāthaḥ (asi) + aśubhaṃ kutaḥ (syāt) = tvayi nāthe, aśubhaṃ kutaḥ

Origin of participles

25. (s + v) + the same s or its pronoun in various cases + v = participle in various cases + v

bālo gacchati + bālo roditi = gacchan bālo roditi
bālo gacchati + taṃ paśyāmi = gacchantaṃ bālaṃ paśyāmi
bālo gacchati + tasmai dadāmi = gacchate bālāya dadāmi, etc. etc.
bālo' gacchat + bālo nāgacchat = gatavān bālo nāgacchat
bālo' gacchat + tam apaśyam = gatavantaṃ bālam apaśyam, etc. etc.
bālo jagāma + bālo mamāra = jagmivān bālo mamāra
bālo jagāma + tasmai dhanam adām = jagmuṣe bālāya dhanam adām, etc.etc.

We can go on combining clauses and turning all but the last verbs into participles, because one sentence can have only one finite verb. Let us see:

1. putro roditi + 2.taṃ pitā nādriyate + 3. pitā pravrajati rudantaṃ putraṃ pitā nādriyate + pitā pravrajati (1-v → participle) ru. pu. anādṛtya pitā pravrajati (2-v → absolutive) rudutaḥ putrasya pitā pravrajati (absol. taken out, making the first clause absolute with the genitive form of the s and the participle).

Another example:

viṣa-vṛkṣam api saṃvardhayati + svayaṃ chetsyati + icchati
= viṣa-vṛkṣam api saṃvardhya svayaṃ chetsyati + icchati (1-v → absolutive)
= viṣa vṛkṣam api saṃvardhya svayaṃ chettum icchati (2-v → infinitive)
viṣa-vṛkṣam api saṃvardhya svayaṃ chettum icchati.
passive = viṣavṛkṣo'pi saṃvardhya svayaṃ chettum iṣyate : Kālidāsa simply turned "na iṣyate" into

asāmpratam, obscuring the passive character of the sentence.

26. (s + o + v-Imp./Opt./Future)-Passive + (the same subject or object or its pronoun in various cases + v) = s → instr. + o → nom. + v-gerundive (participle) in various cases of its s or its pronoun of the following clause + v: sa pustakaṃ paṭhatu/paṭhet/paṭhiṣyati passive : tena pustakaḥ paṭhyatām/paṭhyeta/paṭhiṣyate + sa me rocate = tena paṭhitavyaḥ/paṭhanīyaḥ/pāthyaḥ pustako me rocate.

-do- + tam icchāmi = tena paṭhitavyaṃ pustakam icchāmi

-do- + tasmai spṛhayāmi = tena paṭhitavyāya pustakāya sp ṛhayāmi

-do- + tasya mūlyam = tena pāṭhyasya pustakasya mūlyam

Later the participles themselves assumed the offices of the finite verbs : sa gatavān, gataḥ, jagmivān; tena gantavyam, etc.

19

Some Texts

a. The spider-sign
b. The ant-sign
c. The dog-sign
d. The tail-sign
e. The hindleg-sign
f. The eye-sign
g. The bee-sign
h. The hare-sign
i. The ascetic-sign

a. The spider-sign

It has been normalised as  and occurs 19 times in the inscriptions, as compiled by Mahadevan, but it has four variants, drawn remarkably. They are 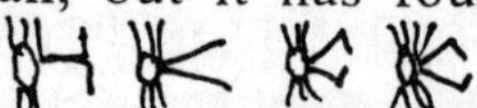

The spider-sign appears to represent the b-syllable (cf. baḥ pumān... tantu-santāne, that is, ba = spider), but it is difficult to replace other vowels for ba.

In the composite sign  ,we may see the diacritic for u, so that it may be read bu. But the four variants,noted above, may represent any one of ba, bi, be, bo for each of them.

The text no. 4280  perhaps reads bo u tū to become botū through Sandhi in course of time. It appears to be a passive clause, subject + verb + object, because ba/bo = he-goat and tū = dog (in some rustic dialect) Referring to it, the RV 1,161,13 says:

> suṣupvāṃsa ṛbhavas tad apṛchatā gohya : ka idaṃ no abūbudhat, śvānaṃ basto bodhyhitāram abravīt saṃvatsara idam adyā vyakhyat.

"O ṛbhus, while asleep you had asked : Agohya, who has awakened us ? The he-goat named the dog to be the awakener. At (the end of) the year, one saw it today."

The he-goat sign (meṣa = Aries) begins with the dog-star Aśvinī (for the original śunī), which marked the beginning of the year at that epoc of the RV.

It appears that the Indus clause also very indirectly says: the new year begins when the sun is at the first degree of the dog-star in the goat-sign on the equinox day.

b. The ant-sign

It has been normalised as . It occurs only seven times but has, nevertheless, six variants. 

Because the number of texts is so small, each variant can be shown in the respective text.

The ant-sign appears to represent the c-syllable, because cīṭī (ant) of Hindi and other regional languages appears to reflect in this symbol. Those c-symbols may be : ca ci cu ce co (short and long), but their identification among the sign-variants is not an easy task. Because diphthongs like cai, etc. can be made by ligaturation, these syllables are restricted to the simple vowels.

All the texts are copied down with the respective variants:

1.  ci 1182 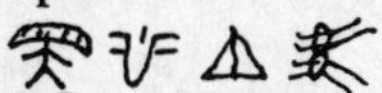 ci h̲- ṣu -ra
2. 8120 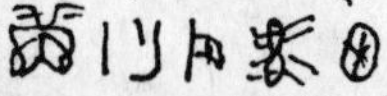 ci ci ra nda la ṣṭha
3.  cī 2002 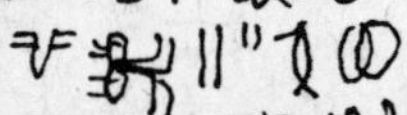 cha jña h̲a ra cī ṣa
4.  cu 2117 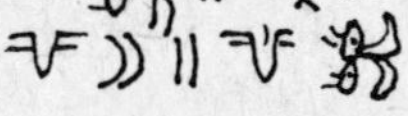 cu ṣu ra ṇa ṣa

5.  cū 2451 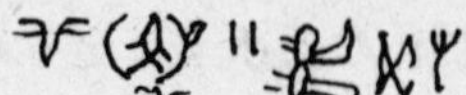 ṇa i cū h̲a niṃ ṣa
6.  ? 4290  ? c- ṣṭha
7.  ? 9801 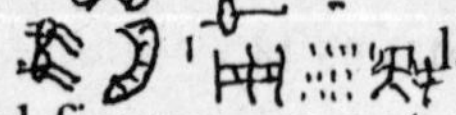 la -da śa - da - c-

Because the animal figures are not generally prepared to take the diacritical marks, the different vowels attached with the consonants represented by them are shown by slightly changing the shape.

The attempts to read the ant-signs phonemically are only provisional, based on guess.

The first text is unreadable on at least three syllables. It is totally illegible.

If the second text consists of three clauses and the first syllable rhymes with the second, we may read them thus:

ci ci ra nda la ṣṭha

If the third text is read ra cī ṣa towards the end, it reflects in a Sanskrit word ṛcīṣa (a frying pan).

The fourth text reads ra ṇa ṣa towards the end. Its c-syllable can be read cu to rhyme with the following ṣu.

The central clause of the fifth text reads cū ha if it reflects in cūhā (a house-rat), which literally means 'making the cū-sound'.

On the basis of ca ṣṭha  elsewhere, the ant-sign may be read ca in the sixth text.

On the basis of  read ṇo rhyming with 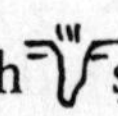 ṣo elsewhere, the ant-sign can be read co in the seventh text.

If the reading of the texts has been difficult, the interpretation is not less so.

c. The dog-sign

It has been normalised as . It occurs eight times and has four variants. They are: 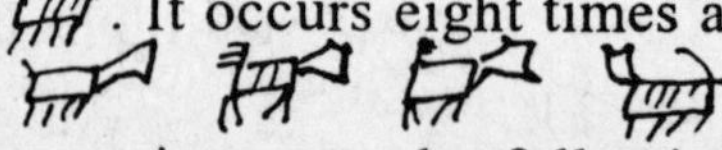

The full texts with the four variants are the followings:

1.	2527	la ḍha gha
2.	3118	ḍo ra ḍhu ṣa
3.	2313	- ḍh- -
4.	1544	ḍh- - h̲a pa ni ha -.

The first text has been taken up for examination elsewhere, and it was found that the whole text has fossilised as ṛdhak, meaning (adv.) 'aside, alone, particularly' in the RV. The transitional stage should have been *ra dha gha, and the meaning of the original clause (time sound emphasis) should have been possibly this: the time bangs indeed, that is, the time signals its march, the time is occasionally remarkable.

This appears to be one of the earliest inscriptions, when gha had not developed its future sense. This variant of the dog-sign thus stands for ḍha.

Just before taking up the second text, we must examine a rare Vedic vocable ṛdu-, generally equated with mṛdu (soft), without any phonetic justification, in the following three compounds: ṛdūdára (mild), ṛdūpā (bee) and ṛdūvṛdh (increasing by sweet).

Because, in the second text, the dog-sign is preceded by ra, we are inclined to read the three signs together as ra ḍhu ṣa. Just as the Indus ṭha has transited into Vedic as ta, ḍhu may have been dentalised and deaspirated as du, and from the possible *ṛdus we can easily imagine a reduced ṛdu-. The first sign of this text represents some ḍ-syllable, probably ḍo, making a clause *ḍo ra (fossilised as the colloquial ḍol 'bucket') meaning 'in the pot (the water) is poured'.

The original clause (speed sound embryo) perhaps means : the movement causes sound, referring to the flowing of some liquid. The sense of 'mildness' would have come from the flowing liquid.

The third and the fourth texts are obscure. It is guessed

that either of the dog-signs represent either ḍhe or ḍho. The eight occurrences of the dog-sign may be thus distributed among ḍha, ḍhu and ḍhe/ḍho.

On the basis of 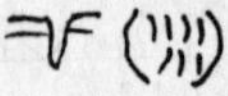 read ḍho ṣa we may suppose that in the following texts the dog-sign reads ḍho :

2305 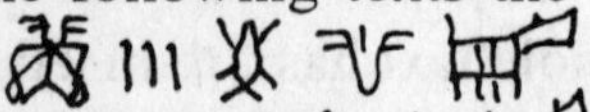 ḍho ṣu ha ta ṣṭha

2219  ḍho ṣu - - - ṣa

The other two texts may have ḍhe value for the dog-sign:

1150 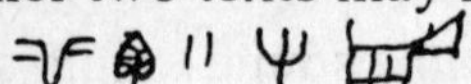 ḍhe ṇa h̲a po ṣa

1099 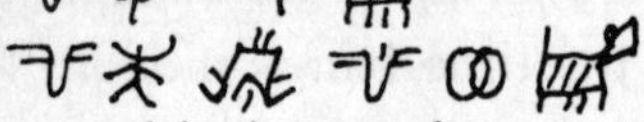 ḍhe cha ṣu bu gra ṣa

Of course, this is purely speculative, without any firm support

d. The tail-sign

The following two texts have this tail-sign, if it is really a tail-sign :

1194 

2442 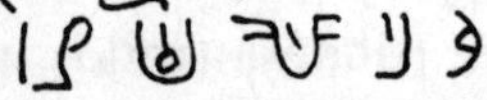

In both these texts it has been drawn differently to show that the consonant represented by it has a different vowel in each case.

The first text has been examined elsewhere, where it has been read śa (injury) pha (abscess) ja (birth), meaning 'through injury abscess is caused'. The whole clause is not seen fossilised anywhere, but the first two syllables make śapha (hoof). Perhaps śa pha themselves make a phrase 'abscess through injury', which began to refer to the instrument of injury, namely the 'hoof'. It is rather more probable that śa itself means 'hoof' and śapha means 'an abscess caused by hoof', which was later restricted to hoof itself.

It is supposed that every syllable of the Indus language, which was a word itself, theoretically amounting to 34 consonants multiplied by 14 vowels = 476, referred to separate items of the different spheres of life. For example, if it referred to the animal world, possibly all of them were comprehended by 476 syllables; if it referred to the world of the birds, all of them were comprehended by 476 syllables, and so on. Thus śa might stand for 'hoof', ṭa for leg, da for tooth, and so on.

The first tail-sign stands for the syllable pha meaning 'abscess'.

It is also here that the bat-sign  has been identified as ja (in jatu 'bat').

The first part of the second text reads : ni nda ṣu. It is a clause syntactically related with the following one, which perhaps reads gau ph- la. The central ph-syllable is still dark. As a matter of fact, the ph-sound seems to express 'split, abscess, swelling, inflammation, fainting, etc. as seen through the Sanskrit and vernacular words.

On the basis of the following la, we can say that this syllable is phū. The whole clause reads : gau phū la.

In the countryside, if an animal eats a certain young plant, it faints fatally and recovers only when an incantation is uttered into its ears for a long time. In that incantation, at least the syllable gau is heard.

With this background, we may interpret the text thus : ni (in the ear) nda (sweet-voice) ṣu (embryo), gau (animal) phū (swoon) la (time). It seems to say : if the sweet voice is put into the ear, the swoon of the animal disappears.

It is probably the text of the veterinary hospital of the urban Indus society.

e. The hindleg-sign

This sign has been normalised as . It occurs eight times and has five variants, which may be seen in the following texts :

1. 3083 
   4683 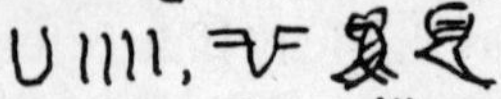
2. 4227 
   8054 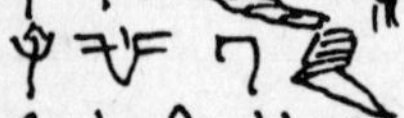
3. 2614 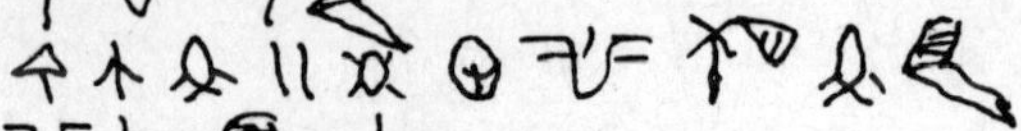
   2152 
4. 1289 
5. 2527 

The last of the texts has been noticed earlier with the dog-sign.

In the fourth text, the hindleg-sign perhaps represents lu to rhyme vocally with the following ṣu. Because there are ṣu and ṣa (reconstructed) in the same line, the two clauses are syntactically related: if/as/when there is la, in h̲a there is da. This is the outline of the meaning. The meaning hinges on the ideas related with la (time) and da (mountain).

The second clause h̲a da ṣa has fossilised as sádas 'seat', dual sadasī 'heaven and earth'. The clause literally means: 'in the empty space there was a mountain'. The whole text perhaps says : as time arose, there was heaven in the sky. It can also mean: as the time rolled, the heaven emerged in the sky.

Though the time and space are twin concepts and arose simultaneously, the other members of the space emerged one by one. There was already some division in time : the past was already gone, the present was there, and the future was gradually emerging.

It also appears that different oblique cases are indicated by bending the vowels towards u, i, e and o.

The latter part of the first text is already understood : la ṭha = the time rolled on, the time turned round. It has fossilised as ṛtá 'the regular order of the universe' with a number of related meanings.

It is preceded by two bisyllabic clauses : dra ṇa h̲a r-
The first and fourth syllables, having r-consonant, have been read only provisionally. If dṛn, an interjection, has any authority, the first two signs, read dra ṇa, may have been reduced to dṛn. Then dra ṇa perhaps means : the hot-fire (sun) activates (life). The following clause perhaps reads h̲a ri, meaning : in the sky there is light.

The RV has two versions of ari : 1. devout, faithful 2. enemy, possibly from two sources. The first meaning may have emerged from h̲a ri (if read correctly).

The text no. 4683 in two lines 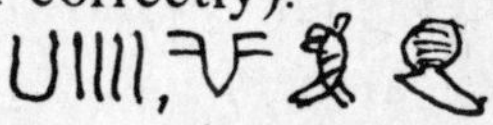 may be read thus : la śa ṣa, ya ga. Before coming to interpret it, let us imagine its fossilised form: the first syllable la may have undergone rhotacism and then reduced to ṛ, the whole text fossilising as *ṛśas. Its further reduced form ṛśa, also extended as ṛśya, stands for a goat-antelope, often portrayed on Indus seals.

The text appears to give the meaning : the hindleg causes injury; take care. This meaning may take us back to the hunting profession in the Indus society.

f. The eye-sign

The eye-sign, normalised as , has eight occurrences in all, but has three variants : 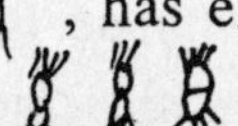. Because the Vedic akṣi (eye) appears to be the fossilised form of some

Indus clause *a ka ṣi (the eyes give joy), we may suppose that the eye-sign stands for a in the Indus syllabary.

The Sanskrit grammarians see a vowel at three lengths : short, long and protracted. Those three variants of the eye-sign probably represent the short, long and protracted a. Probably the geometrical form of the eye-sign is for a and for ā, with no protracted variety.

This is not the case just with respect to a. Even , conceived as i, has a long form in , and probably also protracted form in Of course, it comes under the geometrical figures. The short i is also employed diacritically in ri. If we come to the animal figures, (the horns of some animal) is for i, which is lengthened as , and probably there is no protracted form.

Probably the bow-sign with the arrow put on it is for u, and its length is shown by , with no protracted u. Its geometrical form was (not existent, but imagined through the diacritic in yu) with no long or protracted form traceable.

Though the eye-signs may be read as the short a, long ā and the protracted ā3, it is difficult to identify them in the texts. Some texts are damaged. The undamaged texts are the following:

4701
4345
1421
2125

The final a may be protracted, because in Sanskrit the final vowel of a clause is said to be acutely accented and protracted. An a in the middle or at the initial position may be either long or short. Probably a at the initial position is short.

g. The bee-sign

The bee-sign, supposed to represent the bh-sound, has 130 occurrences, but it has just three variants. We have discovered that the variants are meant to show the same consonants with different vowels. But the variants of the bee-sign are not very remarkable, being the variation caused by the different hands.

There are five simple vowels in Indus, namely a, i, u, e and o, their length being not very significant. Of these simple vowels, a is inherently present in every consonant. To show the vowel u, a small stroke is added to a sign; to show i a similar double stroke is added. There are, rarely, even for o and for e. There are also 5 to 8 such strokes, but we cannot be sure about their values.

The geometrical version of the bh-sound is 7, and there is also 7 with a stroke for bhu. Its numeral variety is 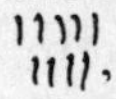, with a capped form 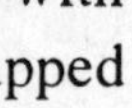 for bhu itself.

We do not see syllables other than bha and bhu in the Indus inscriptions :

h. The hare-sign

This sign has been normalised as . It has 105 occurrence and has 7 variants. The variants are so remarkable that they cannot be ignored as having been written by different hands.

It has been supposed to represent the ś-sound, and in the early Vedic language it is seen to bear the vowels a i u (short and long) e o. Because a is inherent in every consonant, i ī u ū e o may have spread over the six other variants.

The following texts, however, are not identifiable with any Vedic vocable. Only the last śī gha ṣa seems to reflect in śikṣā (the science of phonetics). The Indus text means: the strike causes sound.

Its geometrical version, 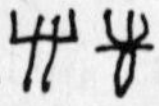 in duplicate, has 4 variants : 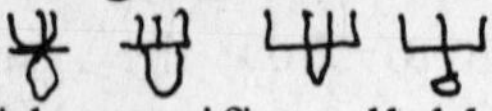 . But it is difficult to identify them with specific syllable.

i. The ascetic sign 

The ascetic sign, in its simple form, occurs only 16 times, but with ribs it occurs 168 times and has 9 variants, not only by diminishing or increasing the number of ribs but also by changing its shapes.

It is supposed to represent the dh-phoneme, and its geometrical version  has 12 variants. Though some of the veriants are the results of the different hands, we are perhaps right in assuming, as a matter of principle, that any remarkable change in shape stands for different vowel related with the same consonant.

About the list of variants in Mahadevan it may be remarked that even some minor variation, which may be due to the different hands of the scribes, have been noted. Whenever it is a major variation, it is certainly a syllable with a different vowel. But any difference in the number of strokes seems to have no importance.

SOME BISYLLABIC CLAUSES

a. ending with dh

b. rau ra

c. ending with ṇa

ka dha 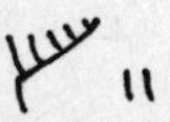

ka dha h̲a pa la 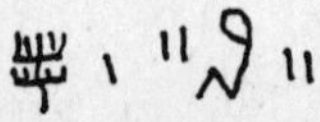

Macdonell does not think that kath 'to say' is an original

root. Its late occurrence has prompted him to think that it is a denominative from kathā = katháṁ (how?), meaning 'to tell how'. The adverb kathā = katháṁ itself is supposed to have been derived from the pronominal base ka- 'who, what'. We may seriously doubt the pronominal origin of a verbal root.

The Indus texts quoted above, though semantically completely obscure, induce us to examine at least the phonetic connection. The first text ka dha and the first part ka dha h̲a of the next may be seen in kathā through the devoicing of the second syllable. The voiceless h may have turned into the laryngeal H and lengthened the preceding vowel.

If these clauses are buried semantically in kathā, we can try to interpret the texts. The two identical clauses may not be having identical meanings, because in the first clause there may be s + v, and in the next there may be either s + o + v or the oblique-case + s + v.

As a matter of fact, if kathā (story, talk) is 'a flash of idea in mind', ka dha may be taken to mean : the moon shines. Its turning into 'a flash of idea' (because the moon is said to have been born from mind) and then its transition into 'saying something orally' (because cakṣ 'to see' later also means 'to say') at the third generation of the language is not surprising. Perhaps the noun kathā (story) has evolved from the clause ka dha.

It may be then assumed that the adverb kathā = katháṁ (how?) is certainly derived from the pronominal base ka-, but the noun kathā is an old vocable recorded very late in the language.

However, the text ka dha h̲a pa la remains to be interpreted. Because the first part is a three-word clause comprising either s + o + v or the oblique-case + s + v, it may mean : the moon emits light, or from the moon the light is emitted. Then the second part pa (plant) la (time) perhaps says : the plants mature. The whole text seems to say : As the moon emits light on them, the plants grow (The plants grow through the light of the moon).

The clause pa la itself may have contracted as -pala in utpala 'lotus', or the root pṛ 'to spread' may be seen in its fossilised form.

There are five or more such two-word clauses ending with dha, namely : ca dha, ja dha, ṭa dha, ḍha dha, and ta dha.

Roth and others derive tathya (truth) and vi-tatha (false) from the pronominal adverb tathā (in that way), but it is difficult to accept this secondary derivation. Like kathā from the Indus clause ka dha, we may assume some *tatha from the Indus clause ta dha.

The meaning of this clause may be based on tathya and vitatha themselves, which point to some 'shining object, abstract or concrete'. Thus, while 'the gem shines' may be one of the obvious meanings even 'virtue' or 'merit' may come to replace the 'gem'. That is to say, tathya and vitatha are related to some obsolete *tatha 'a clear or shining object'.

With the affricate value of /c/ in ca dha, we may come to śad (1. to excel 2. to fall down) and its devoiced form śat (to strike down) in śat-ru, etc., ca having its real meaning lurking in 'thief, mischievous'. Perhaps ca dha = an evil man outshines (a simple man).

The bisyllabic text ḍha dha  has perhaps fossilised as dhat in the Hindi phrase "dhat tere kī", showing disgust, anger, etc. Perhaps ḍha (dog, sound) dha (light) says : the (barking) dog terrifies or frightens. Because our vocabulary of the isolating Indus is uncertain semantically, even though easily identifiable, we are not always sure of the intended meaning. But if one syllable is rightly understood, the other becomes meaningful.

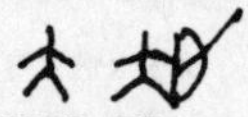

rau ra

This text was read just at the initial stage of decipherment (From Indus to Sanskrit, Pt. II p. 45). It reflects in a Vedic vocable rūrá 'hot' (in opposition to śīta 'cool') qualifying fever (AV 5,22,10), which may help in its interpretation. This text was also responsible for the identification of some other signs.

Though the syllable ra is said to stand for 'fire', other syllables from r may stand for some burning or shining objects. Perhaps rau stands for 'sun', and rau ra seems to say : the sun burns (=is very hot). A very late vocable raurava 'a kind of hell' seems to be just the extension of this primitive clause as rau ra va 'the sun is very hot and strong' or the phrase rau-ra va' a hot sun in the dwelling'. The degeneration of this meaning 'a kind of hell' is easily imaginable. The first part of rūrá 'hot' is available in Hindi lū 'the sunstroke' or in Latin luna 'moon'.

The sign  , having  u from two sides of  ra, may be read either raū or rāu. Because raū is foreign to Sanskrit, it is most likely to be rāu. The sign-group 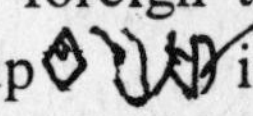 in a longer text may be read rāu ci which, with the affricate value of /c/ may have become lutti 'a spark of the fire' colloquially.

The syllable rau, followed by the injunctive ga, is necessarily a verb · let it burn. Perhaps the Vedic róga 'disease' has evolved from rau gha (a future form 'will burn') in the clause 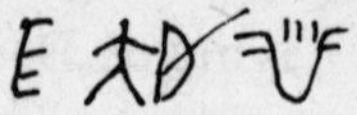 ṣo rau gha. Otherwise, rau is mostly a noun, some burning or shining object, specifically 'the sun'.

Some bisyllabic clauses ending with ṇa

Pāṇini (4,1,7) refers to (a) n changing into r, and (b) colloquially even today n is heard pronounced as r or l in some words. There are also some words (c) having l in place of n from an unknown period :

(a) śarvan becomes f. śarvar-ī (night)

(b) nārāyaṇa is pronounced larāyan colloquially

(c) *Nānandā has been Nālandā (a town) since its recorded history.

That is to say, there is a very ancient phonetic tendency of the nasal n changing into r or l. This prompts us to examine some verbs ending with ṛ in Sanskrit as to its origin from some original n.

The word maṇi (gem) and the verb mar (to shine) in mar-u (sand), mar-ut (the shining deity Marut) appear to be distantly connected, at least semantically. Even mar-ya (a young handsome lad) is derived from this mar, and mar-ta too (cf. Persian mard) is derived from the same mar, though in mṛta 'dead' cf. Persian murd) the meaning has deviated.

If this mar (to shine) is supposed to have emerged from some *man, there is actually a bisyllabic text ma ṇa 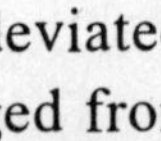 in the Indus inscriptions, which probably means 'the moon shines' or 'in the moon there is light'. Because ma means also 'death', mar used reflexively (mriyate) means 'to die'.

The clause ma ṇa may have come together as the phrase *mana, from which the verb mar 'to shine' or 'to die' could have been deduced. A slightly different meaning of the clause ma ṇa, namely 'in the moon there is intelligence', may be the basis of the verse 'candramā manaso jātaḥ' (the moon was born from the mind).

Another reduced form of the phrase *mana is the rare vocable mán 'ornament' (RV 8,78,2), though it is a ghost word of the most radical Vedic disctionaries.

The Indus text pa ṇa  perhaps means 'in the plant (there is) life'. The phrase *pana later evolved as par (pṛ) 'to spread', though there are even paṇ and pan versions of the verb with different meanings.

The verb jar (jṛ) 'to grow old' may have evolved from the text ja ṇa 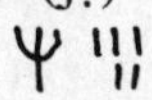, which perhaps means 'in the birth there is death'.

The text dha ṇa 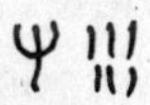 may have evolved as dhar (dhṛ) in the reflexive dhriyate 'to be alive'. This text perhaps means : in the heat there is life.

Similarly, the text ta ṇa 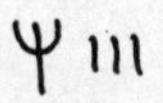 perhaps means: in the womb there is life. From the phrase *tana the verb tar (tṛ) may have been derived. The verb tar originally means : to go into another stage.

In the same way, the Indus texts gha ṇa 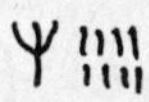, ca ṇa ṭa ṇa 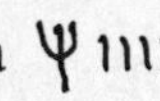, ṭha ṇa 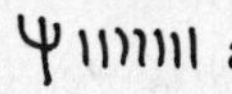 and ḍha ṇa 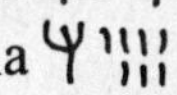 may be the source of many Sanskrit roots with ṛ :

ghan	:	ghṛ 'to drip'
can	:	car 'to move'
ṭan	:	ṭar/l (Hindi) 'to deviate'
ṭhan	:	ṭhar 'to shiver'
ḍhan	:	ḍhar 'to pour'

20

How a Man Began Speaking

I conclude this book with my views on the origin of the human speech, in spite of the ban imposed by the linguists.

The long protracted bellowing of a bull or buffalo, the roaring of a lion or tiger, or the cry of little animals was reduced in length, as it were, when it passed on to the clucking of the monkeys. It was further cut down in length as it passed on to the babbling of a caveman. The first human utterance was some vague sound or just some noise upto the length of what we may call 'three mātrās' : ā3, ī3, ū3*, etc. These three mātrāic noises were the socalled vowels, appropriately called svara (noise) by the Sanskrit grammarians. They were further cut down to two mātrās, then to just one mātrā. Thus the first sounds produced by the human beings were the socalled vowels of the three lengths, namely short, long and protracted.

At a later stage, after the long protracted noise climbed down to a measurable length, a soft or hard breathing (h) came to precede the socalled vowels. Hermann Beckh (Neue Wege zur Ursprache, p. 23f) had perhaps rightly perceived it. This was the beginning of the articulate human sounds, later appropriately called Vyañjana by the Sanskrit grammarians. It is not surprising to find that the syllable ha has more than a score of meanings in the traditional Sanskrit lexicons of the monosyllabic words. Perhaps even soft or hard hissing sounds (z s) preceded the vowel at the same time. It was followed by the nasals of various origins. These breathing and hissing sounds as well as nasals too were originally continuants, but they were cut short by the following vowels as soon as they were uttered : ha hā hā3, si sī sī3, mu mū mū3.

The next products of the human vocal organs, now able to strike like lightning, were the voiced and voiceless explosives, followed by the corresponding aspirates, the voiced or the voiceless breathing (h) immediately, almost integrally, following the plain stops.

The origin of the diphthongs (ai āi au āu) and affricates (dz ts) is the result of later clustering, sometimes integrally (j c). The continuant l and the trilled r would have originated sometime between the consonants and the vowels.

The order of the human sounds thus produced would have been like this, which may be called the ur-Māheśvarasūtras, but the original order was edited and updated when ṛ l developed from ra la at the inflexional stage and e o went out of use at the high time of the Vedic language. Though Pāṇini still saw the diphthongs in their original form, he pronounced them as e ai o au. He pronounced the short vowel A with the closed (saṃvṛta) mouth with three mātrās, though he spoke his grammar with its 'open' value.

His e and o were long, not corresponding to their short ĕ ŏ but because they had contracted from the diphthongs ai au. The original e o were out of use long before Pāṇini.

---

* A cock is said to utter ku with all the three mātrās, that is, ku kū kū3.

The Indus phoneticians had also marked the relative frequencies of the sounds of the language at the isolating stage. A look at the syllabic order of the ur-Māheśvarasūtras shows that the simple vowels were more frequent than the diphthongs, the short vowels more so than the long ones. The voiceless h was more frequent than the voiced one, and the lateral l more frequent than the trilled r. The semivowel v was more frequent than y, corresponding to u i among the vowels. The voiceless stops were more frequent than the voiced ones, and the aspirates were far less numerous than the unaspirates, the voiceless aspirates other than ṭh being almost negligible. The voiceless unaspirates competed among themselves for their superior presence in the language. As long as k g and c j were near each other at velum and soft palate, they also interchanged.

The Sanskrit grammarians never realised that the palatal stops were once also affricates; they did not know that jān (āmi) was dān- in old persian. Therefore, they considered the interchange of the velars and palatals (kuhoś cuḥ : coḥ kuḥ) in wordformation as a natural process. Though the RV-Prātiśākhya says that the dentals are alveolars, they are purely dental to Pāṇini. It may be then supposed that they were gradually replacing the cerebrals, which were obstinately retained in the Dravidian languages. We now understand the cause of the paucity of the cerebrals in Sanskrit. As the Aryans proceeded towards the west, the cerebrals were completely wiped out. The cerebrals were not introduced to Sanskrit but they were lost from it.

We already know how Sanskrit evolved from Indus.